A GAME THAT FORGED RIVALS

To Luciano My favorite Restauranteur! — And football FAN

MARK C. BODANZA

10/2/09

iUniverse, Inc.

New York   Bloomington

A Game That Forged Rivals
How Competition between Two New England High Schools
Created One of the Greatest Traditions in Football

iUniverse books may be ordered through booksellers or by contacting:

iUniverse
1663 Liberty Drive
Bloomington, IN 47403
www.iuniverse.com
1-800-Authors (1-800-288-4677)

ISBN: 978-1-4401-5648-9 (pbk)
ISBN: 978-1-4401-5646-5 (cloth)
ISBN: 978-1-4401-5647-2 (ebook)

Printed in the United States of America

iUniverse rev. date: 8/25/09

To my father and greatest teacher,
Rosario Bodanza,

and

to the grandson of Mark L. O'Toole,
Coach Michael Curley

Contents

Preface

I have always had a keen interest in history, savored good traditions, and been passionate about football. Why it hadn't occurred to me to write this book sooner, I'm not sure. However, the Leominster-Fitchburg rivalry certainly combines those elements which have provided me a great deal of pleasure. Over the last decade, pursuit of the local past has led me to the discovery of a rich bounty of primary historical sources. In many cases, yellowed documents, worn bindings, and curled, fading photographs lay undisturbed for many years. The chronicles contained in these aging repositories deserve to be told.

I was confident the history of Fitchburg and Leominster football involved accounts no less compelling. In a very short time, my research uncovered an abundance of human experiences that had occurred both on and off the football field. The rivalry defied challenges to its very existence and endured remarkable changes, both within the sport and to America itself. It became apparent that even the most ardent of contemporary high school football fans could find something novel and fascinating in the early origins of the Leominster-Fitchburg football tradition.

This book was started on a smaller scale. Initially, the project was intended as a program to accompany a recreation of the rivalry's first game of 1894, an event scheduled to take place on October 24, 2009. However, the volume and intensity of the subject could not be constrained to such a limited treatment. I examined countless newspaper articles, school yearbooks, game programs, eyewitness accounts, letters, photographs, and archival records. Each resource underscored the need to undertake an assembly of both the essential thread of the rivalry and, more importantly, a context for the series and for the generations that perpetuated its drama.

Football is a great sport. Over and over again, the analysis of local football history illustrates the dramatic nature of the game. Its earliest pioneers, including the father of American football, Walter Camp, recognized it to be a game of brain and brawn. That sentiment is undeniable; however, football is also a game of heart.

I didn't have to look very far for an example of how emotion plays a part in football. One of football's most inspirational stories is credited to involve Leominster's own Lou Little, a legendary college football coach at both Georgetown and Columbia. While coaching at Georgetown, Little attempted to excuse a bench-riding substitute from a game after the player's dad had suddenly died. The young man declined the leave and instead asked the coach the favor of participating in just one play. Little, who could not refuse, agreed and sent the young man out on the kickoff team. To the amazement of Coach Little and the team, the fellow made a blistering tackle deep in the opponent's territory. Little left him in the game, and he turned in an astounding fifteen unassisted tackles. The coach, who couldn't explain what he witnessed, knew he had misjudged this young man. As the locker room emptied, the coach and underestimated player sat alone. The coach attempted to apologize for his prior lack of confidence. The young man interrupted, reminding the coach that his departed dad was blind but, on that day, his father was able to see him play football for the first time.

Football will always be played with heart. The high schools of Fitchburg and Leominster have sent thousands of young men to the gridiron who have played the game in that very way. This book is my attempt to honor their exploits and the beliefs they shared for their community, schools, and this special football rivalry.

Acknowledgments

Researching and writing local history has been rewarding. Modern historians have come to realize that the fabric of the past cannot be fully appreciated by a study of national iconic figures only. It has been my pleasure to be surrounded by many people with a great deal of enthusiasm for local history.

I am particularly indebted to my friend, Nancy Bell, who provided invaluable critiques of the early manuscript, a great deal of encouragement, and the inspiration to consider the possibilities of the book. Acclaimed author and Leominster native, Adrian Nicole LeBlanc, provided valuable insight and support. Lifelong friends Brian Montaquila and Peter Angelini were there to listen and add thoughts during many discussions as the manuscript progressed. My editor, Kathi Wittkamper, was always informative, supportive, and a delight to work with.

My research was facilitated by a number of organizations and helpful individuals. Thanks to the Leominster Historical Society and especially Jane Fischer and Sandra Balboni; also Linda Pinder, who provided her considerable talents to the photographic contributions. The Fitchburg Historical Society, its director, Susan Roetzer, and staff members were gracious and supportive hosts. Likewise, Tom Shea provided great assistance during my visit to the Crocker Field House. My friends at the Leominster Public Library, including Director Susan Shelton, valuable collection coordinator Jeannine Levesque, and staff were, as always, cooperative and welcoming.

I am thankful to many individuals who contributed photos, game programs, yearbooks, and more importantly, their memories. Riccardo Cavaioli, a member of Leominster's 1932 undefeated team, welcomed me to his home and his wonderful reminiscences. Connie Curley shared her enthusiasm for the game and memorabilia from the O'Toole family. Leominster's athletic director, Chris Young, and Fitchburg's coach, Ray Cosenza, added recollections from the 1993 edition of the rivalry.

My good friend Coach Michael Austin and his brother Lewis Austin shared their engaging love for the game. Sadly, Lewis Austin passed away only a few weeks after recounting the memorable end to the 1978 Thanksgiving game.

I owe a debt of gratitude to Richard O'Brien, central director of the Trustees of Reservations, for his belief in this project and for permitting the recreation to take place on the grounds of the historic Doyle Estate. A special thank you goes to Jack Celli and Carl Piermarini for their significant contributions to preserving the local past, participating in this project, and paving the way with their documentary film *The Rivalry*. I wish to thank my parish priest, Father James Callahan, and Principal Danielle Colvert for the use of St. Anna's school gym, where we first witnessed nineteenth-century football live and in color. Gilbert and Maureen Donatelli were early and significant supporters of the game recreation, which helped in immeasurable ways. Joe and Lisa DeCarolis and Andrew and Patricia Rome supported efforts to recreate nineteenth-century football.

The administrative staff of my law office, Kathleen Welch and Gabriella Goodale, cheerfully helped, as they are always willing to do. My brother and law partner, David Bodanza, gave his unending support, which will always be one of my greatest blessings.

Finally, I offer my love and appreciation to my wife, Adele, and children Melissa, Kathryn, and Nicholas for their support, understanding, and patience.

Introduction

The word *rivalry* has its origin in the Latin *rivalis,* which means "a person using the same stream as another." From their founding, the communities of Leominster and Fitchburg have shared the same river. In one town, the river drops precipitously, more than eight hundred feet, while in the other it rolls gently, flattening as it passes through enriched soils once farmed by the native peoples. The river takes its name from those ancient farmers who made their homes between its two branches. This tribe took the name Nashaway, which translated to "the land between." A little more than two decades after the Pilgrims landed, other English settlers came to trade, settle, and convert the native people to Christianity. By the end of the seventeenth century, the Nashaway tribe had been virtually wiped out by white settlers and the diseases they brought and by powerful rival tribes, the Massachusetts to the east and the Mohawks to the west. When the devastation was complete, all that remained was the river and its name.

Along the banks of the Nashaway, or Nashua River, as the name was also translated, the towns of Leominster and Fitchburg were carved. The inhabitants of each relied on the natural riches God created: hills, forests, fields, and especially the river. The river powered mills in each town and gave birth to the earliest industries of both. In the last decade of the nineteenth century, the high schools of these two New England towns, which had long shared the same river, began one of the greatest modern rivalries in sport. Why these two towns developed a storied football rivalry is not entirely clear. When the ancient series began in 1894, the communities were different in many ways, and the distinctions have continued throughout the years.

Until recently, Fitchburg was the larger community. In their competition for the waters of the Nashua, Fitchburg was the greatest benefactor. The river first passed through Fitchburg and, because of sharply falling waters, that town harnessed much more power than did its neighbor, Leominster. In the first decades of rivalry, Leominster's population was less than half of that of Fitchburg's. The larger community boasted a golden age of industrial, business, and cultural development never witnessed by its smaller neighbor. In most ways, the towns and their high schools were not counterparts. Their rivalry did not spring naturally from like qualities. The long tradition of Leominster and Fitchburg did not have the inevitability of other rivalries like Harvard-Yale or Army-Navy. Nevertheless, the competition between these teams—and not the many other schools each played—became heightened very early.

Before the nineteenth century came to a close, the schools, which from today's vantage were in the infancy stage of their relationship, already referred to each other as "old-time rivals." Leominster was an upstart and Fitchburg was an early target. Fitchburg was more than happy to accommodate.

The young men of Fitchburg and Leominster were local football pioneers in the last decade of the nineteenth century. In a time when horse-drawn transportation was still common, these early football players possessed gridiron dreams, made all the more keen by the fabled examples of Harvard, Yale, Pennsylvania, Princeton, Army, Brown, Dartmouth, and a host of other intercollegiate teams making newspaper headlines each autumn. Early on, local newspapers were proud to exclaim that their local series captured all the excitement of the wildly popular intercollegiate rivalries.

Like independent steeds, those local boys yearned to take to the field in full stride. The imagery of their favorite charger quickly closing the distance of a bucolic pasture was no less pleasing than breaking free on the football field. Those young men, unlike their fathers and grandfathers, were a generation free of war. Football was a way to prove themselves. The nascent sport, introduced at local driving parks and fairgrounds, required an expression of manliness and toughness that suited these football pioneers just right. However, the brutality of the early years of football threatened the very foundation of the sport. Neither mounting serious injuries nor wholesale rule changes would damage the intense desire of Leominster and Fitchburg to compete. Their rivalry would weather dramatic developments in the game, economic turmoil, wars, epidemics, remarkable new technologies, and social changes not imaginable to the first generations, who served as guardians of the rivalry in its earliest decades. Obviously, changes impacted more than just the football rivalry. In many ways, the communities have competed off the field through the years. The question arises: which competition came first, civic pride or football? Leominster citizens looked askance at Fitchburg's commercial and cultural resources, from the late nineteenth century to the middle of the next epoch. Fitchburg's commercial center boasted stores, accommodations, and entertainment not nearly equaled in Leominster.

Leominster's industry, while growing in the first decades of the twentieth century, did not favorably compare to a neighbor that was setting national standards. Football and athletic facilities did not escape comparison either. By the close of World War I, Fitchburg's high school athletic facility was also setting national standards. Leominster had to be content with a second-rate field, barely large enough to accommodate the game itself. Fitchburg refused to play on Leominster's inadequate field.

The disparities were not lost on Leominster's leaders. Leominster's development came at a slower pace. The communities were often compared, something that has persisted until today. After having started out so differently, the communities became known as the "Twin Cities." If that were ever true, it is no longer the case, and the term has fallen into disuse. Over the years, Leominster and Fitchburg have been at odds over things which common borders are bound to cause.

In the early 1990s, the communities disputed, with some additional irony, water. Fitchburg attempted to build an industrial park in the watershed of Leominster's Notown Reservoir. Leominster objected, and at least some local officials deemed the controversy as possessing a "turkey-day mentality." At first blush, the concept of the ancient gridiron competition spilling over into a dispute over goals for infrastructure at the border between communities seems silly. Frivolous or not, the comment demonstrates that the football competition between the two cities is never very far from the surface.

Today, the 114-year-old rivalry seems quite inevitable. The story that follows is how it got to that point. It is the story of the development of football from its earliest form to a game more recognizable to the modern fan. It is a story of two communities that saw, in football, a way to grasp an extra measure of civic pride. It is a story of two communities that struggled to create better institutions and a better economy for their citizens. But most of all, it is a story of people who met challenges both on and off the football field and endured.

Chapter One

The Nation, 1894

It was a pivotal year for America. It was a time of historic importance for football, especially in the New England communities of Leominster and Fitchburg.

In 1894, football held the imagination of the nation's youth while hard economic times took hold of the nation. How high-school-age boys perceived the economic concerns of their parents is merely speculation. Whatever they thought, the country reeled and convulsed from an economic downturn and the political upheaval that always follows a time of great uncertainty. The panic, which had its start in 1893, was a profound economic depression rooted in an overexpansion by the railroads and exacerbated by overextended financing. The federal government issued two large bond offerings in an attempt to alleviate the drain on the treasury. Populist political candidates questioned the power of monopolistic corporations, and striking workers sought more equitable wages. President Grover Cleveland, a Democrat, was blamed for the turmoil. America's industrial muscle spasmed and newspaper headlines captured the somber story.

Before the air turned cool and schools reopened for the new academic year, summer simmered with anticipation of the fall elections. In June of 1894, populist politicians and "Silver Democrats" convened in Omaha, Nebraska to advance a policy of silver and paper money. Silver and paper currency, as opposed to gold, was championed as the money of the common man. Labor and debt-laden farmers saw relief in an expansion of the currency that silver and paper money represented. Simply put, the Silver Democrats wanted the government to print more money to ease the repayment of debt and expand the availability of credit. Republicans, business, and eastern financiers clung to the principle of a sound currency backed by gold, the international standard of trade. William Jennings Bryan, the editor of the *Omaha World-Herald,* addressed the silver convention. Bryan ran for president in 1896 and two additional times, each time on a silver platform and each time unsuccessfully. [1]

Before the midterm elections of 1894, more than six hundred banks and more than twenty-two thousand miles of railroads were in receivership. A quarter of the nation's heavy industrial capacity lay idle. When the unhappy electorate was heard, Republicans made historic gains in both houses of Congress.[2] The Democrats and their president, Grover Cleveland, absorbed the ire of voters concerned about the direction of the American economy while Leominster boys rustled autumn leaves on their way to football practice during the fall of 1894.

In spite of the nation's difficulties, Leominster's industry weathered

---

1   William Jennings Bryan, a devout Baptist and former congress-man, rose to national prominence during the Democratic Convention of 1896, where he received the party's nomination after delivering his famous "cross of gold" speech, which captured the hearts and minds of the Democratic Convention-goers. Bryan famously proclaimed, "You shall not press upon the brow of labor this crown of thorns; you shall not crucify mankind upon a cross of gold." Bryan, who embodied a moral missionary, lost the presidential election of 1896 to William McKinley. The voters were not ready to chance change that McKinley successfully painted as radical reform.

2   President Cleveland cost his party dearly. He was not only disadvantaged by the poor economy, but also his stubborn adherence to the gold standard, which did nothing to court a large portion of his own party that saw silver money as a cure for the economic problems and social injustices.

the economic downturn with a remarkable measure of resiliency. Piano-case companies were founded: Richardson Piano Case Company in 1891 and the Wellington Piano Case Company in 1895. These companies joined previously established firms in an industry that grew and prospered until the Great Depression came and family entertainment was more likely to include a gathering around the radio than the parlor piano. While Leominster's industry chocked smoke and steam into the October dusk, the town's earliest football players hustled to practice at the old militia training field, Carter Park. Leominster's first town center and proving ground once again welcomed a squad of young men ready to hone their skills on the brisk autumn evenings of 1894. Afternoons were reserved for after-school jobs in factories, which several of the high school players had to attend before gridiron maneuvers could be practiced and daydreams of football glory turned to reality.

The American economy would not begin its recovery until 1896, when the election of Republican President William McKinley and the Klondike gold rush helped restore America's confidence. A heady self-assurance, magnified by an attitude that envisioned great possibilities, would ignite a decade of rapid economic expansion once the American economy got back on its feet.

Leominster

The late nineteenth century was a period of dramatic population growth. The 1890 census recorded an American population that had nearly doubled since the start of the Civil War in 1861. A significant portion of this growth was the result of immigration from northern European nations. The fabric of Leominster's 1894 football team was in part woven with the sons of immigrants seeking social inclusion by way of a sport that was no less finished in its development than the assimilation of the human waves arriving at the shore. Mark O'Toole, who would anchor Leominster's line at right tackle during the fall of 1894, was born in Leominster on September 29, 1878. His father, recently arrived from Ireland, sought a promise of opportunity that could not be fulfilled in his native land. Patrick O'Toole was a comb maker living and working in Leominster's Morse Hollow, a neighborhood centered near the intersection of Exchange Street, Birch Street, and the Monoosnock Brook, that employed, housed, and fed more than a hundred comb makers in factories, homes, and a store built by the Morse family. Many of the workers in the factories of Morse Hollow were Irish immigrants. Even today, descendants of those newcomers still live in the homes their fathers built with a gritty determination, hard work, and sacrifice.

Life in New England, especially for the foreign born, was hard in the nineteenth century. Patrick O'Toole died prematurely on December 9, 1887, leaving his widow, Mary (Daley) O'Toole, who was pregnant with their fifth child. Patrick, thirty-nine years old at the time of his death, never realized the dreams he had for his young family. The youngest O'Toole, Ann Frances, was born less than five weeks after her father's death. Mark O'Toole, who was nine at the time of his father's passing, and his four younger sisters grew up with their widowed mother in the family home at 1 Cherry Street. From that address, Mark O'Toole would attend Field High School, form aspirations, and keep faith in possibilities that America never fully revealed to his father. He and four succeeding generations of his family journeyed America's unfolding experience residing in but three homes no farther apart than the length of a football field.

Fitchburg

Fitchburg's depot, from which its football team would depart on October 20, 1894 for a fateful journey to Leominster, was a bustling center, processing passengers and freight on an impressive succession of trains. The rail, as much as the river, transformed Fitchburg from the "turkey hills" of Lunenburg's northwestern hinterland to a center of population and industry. A casual notice in the *Fitchburg Sentinel* was a harbinger of what lay ahead. "The citizens of Fitchburg who feel an interest in the subject of a railroad from this place to the City of Boston are requested to meet at the Town Hall on Friday evening, Nov 19, 1841, at half-past six o'clock, to adopt such measures as they may think proper."[3]

Five decades of rail, river, and entrepreneurial ingenuity brought

---

3   *Fitchburg Sentinel*, November 18, 1841.

breathtaking industrial advances to Fitchburg. The nation celebrated the Columbian Exposition, or Chicago's World Fair, in 1893, commemorating the four hundredth anniversary of Columbus's voyage to the new world. The largest exhibit among the greatest technological displays of the age belonged to Fitchburg's Simonds Saw and Steel Company. Fitchburg's population grew dramatically to keep pace with the demand for labor created by industrial growth. It began modestly when the foreign-born population rose from 1,500 to more than 2,500 on the eve of Fitchburg's graduation to city status in 1872. Between 1890 and 1895, the floodgate was opened. The population rose from 22,037 to 26,409. More than nine thousand of the new total were of foreign birth.[4]

Fitchburg was a diverse place under construction in the later decades of the nineteenth century. Rollstone Hill, shadowing Fitchburg's center, yielded the granite to be cut into architectural elements for new buildings and curbing for streets. The Fitchburg Depot, with its majestic clock tower rising some 128 feet, was trimmed with Fitchburg granite. Artisans as well as laborers were in demand. Henry Godbeer was a stone mason who, along with his wife Sarah, immigrated to Fitchburg in 1871. The Godbeers had five children; two, John and Elizabeth, had been born in Artherington, Devonshire, England. The Godbeers settled in West Fitchburg briefly, where their third child, George Henry Godbeer, was born in 1872. The youngest children, Edith and Clifford, were born in Fitzwilliam, New Hampshire, where the family resided for more than a decade before returning to Fitchburg in 1886.

Upon his return to Fitchburg, Henry Godbeer established the Henry Godbeer Granite Company and a quarry on Rollstone Hill. All of the Godbeer boys tried their hand at the demanding and physical work of their father. Only one brother, John, stayed in the trade and he maintained the granite company well into the twentieth century. George left the family business at age nineteen in 1891 and launched a seventy-year career as a reporter and editor of the *Fitchburg Sentinel*. The youngest brother, Clifford, pursued a career with the railroads. One thing the brothers shared was a deep interest in sports, especially football. The youngest brother, Clifford F. Godbeer, enrolled at

---

4   Kirkpatrick, *Around the World in Fitchburg*, 5.

Fitchburg High School in the fall of 1892. When the trolley car left the depot carrying the Fitchburg High School football team to Leominster in October of 1894, one of the teammates was Clifford Godbeer.[5]

Playing American football was not central to the vision of the families of Mark O'Toole and Clifford Godbeer; however, in the dimming light of a Saturday afternoon in October of 1894, these two young men met at Leominster's driving park for a football game. The game they played that autumn day was not much older than the young men themselves. Football was a developing sport that in some way mirrored the changes in American society.

American sport, in general, was influenced by democratic, industrial, and social changes affecting the nation. The more genteel and rural pleasures of hunting and fishing were not available to an increasingly urban workforce. Yet these urban masses had a thirst for entertainment and sports that provided an outlet for the expression of manliness and strength. Young men, college-bound or not, sought self-improvement that included mental advancement and courage. The football field became a place where young men would come of age and prove some of the most basic qualities that earn a man respect: strength, bravery, and, most importantly, placing team above self. In this milieu, American football was born and reared.

---

5   Kirkpatrick, *Around the World in Fitchburg*, 60.

— *Chapter Two* —

The Birth and Development of Intercollegiate Football through the Mid-1890s

Although the first professional football game was played at Latrobe, Pennsylvania on August 31, 1895, the sport was essentially an intercollegiate one in 1894. By the mid-1890s, American football owed its popularity to fabled rivalries and clashes between football college grid powers. And popular it was; in fact, intercollegiate football was more popular than college baseball by the 1890s.[6] In his 1896 book *Football*, Walter Camp, the father of the American game, wrote:

> This volume is published in the hope that it may aid in the development of American football, and more especially that it may encourage a scientific study of the game. The great popularity of this sport is not without its reasonable warrant. It calls out not merely the qualities which make the soldier—bravery, endurance, obedience, self-control—but equally that mental acumen which makes the successful man in any

---

6   Oates, *The First Fifty Years: The Story of the National Football League*, 212.

of the affairs of life—perception, discrimination, and judgment.

To the casual observer, football doubtless presents merely the spectacle of vigorous physical exercise. But a deeper insight will discover the steady development of those other qualities which make the complete man— quick determination, instant obedience, self-reliance, physical bravery. The great lesson of the game may be put into a single line: *it teaches that brains will always win over muscle!*

It is not drawback to the game that its object is a simple one; when you tell the spectator that each side is trying to reach the opponent's goal, you have stated all that need be said. It is similarly no drawback to its popularity that professional football is unknown in America.

But the great merit of this sport is its practically unlimited field of tactical development. The fascinating study of new movements and combinations is never exhausted. It is this tactical possibility which has elevated football in popular esteem above all other sports. The cause of its attractiveness has its parallel in war. No pages of war history are so interesting to the student as the stirring descriptions of battles in which, by superior direction, a comparatively small body of soldiers has routed a force of twice its strength.

It is on these high lines that the American game of football may be developed. It is in the hope that they may aid that development that the authors print this volume. *September, 1896.*[7]

American football's evolution is traced to 1876 when Harvard and Yale substituted rugby union rules for the Association game, a soccer-

---

7   Camp and Deland, *Football*, iii.

style version of football. Both games had British roots. Britons had been kicking at inflated animal bladders for centuries. Tradition has it that men of colonial New England entertained themselves after Thanksgiving dinner with a game that involved kicking at an inflated pig's bladder.[8]

As the legend is told, in the year 1823, student William Ellis exhilarated spectators at Rugby College England when he tired of kicking at the ball, picked it up and ran with it, in clear violation of the rules. While some scholars dispute that this was the origin of rugby, the college from which the sport takes its name maintains a plaque commemorating the event.

Rugby's popularity in America was owing to the same excitement and rugged style of play produced by a player running with the ball. In rugby, play commences with a "scrum" or "scrummage." Teams gather around the ball, arms and bodies interlocked, and kick at the ball until it is freed from the pack. Once the ball comes out, it is seized by a half-back who in turn passes it to a three-quarter who runs with or kicks the ball.

Almost immediately, American players began to modify play, and more particularly, the operation of the "scrum." Players began to let the opponents do the kicking and instead concentrated on waiting for the opportune moment before kicking the ball to their outlet teammates. As more teams and players became adept at this practice, teams began to roll the ball sidewise between their lines until one of the players could snap the ball back with his toe to his outlet. From these changes came the regularized "snap-back" or center and quarterback.[9]

By 1884, the scrum was replaced by the "line of scrimmage" and a system of three downs to make five yards or lose ten. The rugby rule that prohibited interference (blocking) in front of the ball carrier, not often observed or enforced, was formally repealed by rule in 1888.

---

8   According to Walter Camp, this game was highly informal and was regulated by local rules that were in many cases interpreted on the field. Camp and DeLand, *Football*, 16.

9   Walter Camp, in *American Football*, chronicles the transformation of rugby to football. "At first the play was crude in the extreme, but even in its earliest stages it proved distinctly more satisfactory to both player and spectator than the kicking and shoving which marked the English method." Camp, *American Football*, 11.

Still, some antecedents from rugby continued in American football of the mid-1890s. The quarterback, or the first player to touch the snap from the snapback or center, could not run with the ball until the ball was first handled by another player. The center continued to be referred to as the "snap back," and that player could continue to snap the ball back by his toe as well as the more modern technique of snapping the ball back by means of a pass from his hands.

Much of American's football development during the last two decades of the nineteenth century was the work of Walter Camp, universally referred to as the "father of American football." Camp played for Yale and later coached the team to a number of national championships. He was largely responsible for the adoption of rules that moved American football away from rugby and toward the team-oriented sport that more closely resembles what we today know as football. To be sure, many rule changes loomed, not the least of which was the adoption of the forward pass; however, Camp was clearly the pioneer most responsible for American football.[10] Camp wrote in his 1896 book *Football,* "Coaching football team is the most engrossing thing in the world. It is playing chess with human pawns."[11]

Violence, the Flying Wedge, and Rule Changes in 1894

There were many early inquiries as to the violent nature of football. A committee of Harvard faculty conducted an investigation of the new game in 1884. Their report documented savage fistfights that frequently required the intervention of game officials or the police. The

---

10   In 1894, a forward pass was a foul that carried the penalty of loss of possession at the point of the pass. The pass would not emerge until 1906, and in its initial form was severely restricted. An incomplete pass that was touched was treated as a fumble. An incomplete pass that was not touched resulted in a loss of possession at the point of the pass. A forward pass could be no longer than twenty yards until that restriction was removed in 1912. The pass had to cross the line of scrimmage within five yards of the point at which it was snapped and had to be released at least five yards behind the line of scrimmage.

11   Watterson, *Out of Baseball's Shadow: The Paradox of Football Scholarship,* 221.

faculty also had grave concerns about the conduct of spectators who at times encouraged violence from the players exhorting them to "slug," "kill," or "break the neck" of their opponents. After the conclusion of the 1884 season, the Harvard faculty voted to ban football; however, angry student protests restored the sport by the start of the 1886 campaign.[12]

By the end of the 1880s, the college rules committee sanctioned the art of blocking and tackling below the waist. The official inclusion of interference or blocking in the game signaled an end to the era of individualized play consistent with the former rugby scrum and outlet and toward a team-oriented style of play. It would not be long before football tacticians would develop offensive weapons that would maximize the use of interference.

In 1892, Harvard Coach Lorin F. Deland, a man also recognized for his chess expertise, introduced the "flying wedge." This tactic involved the principle of mass momentum. Several players would assemble behind the line of scrimmage in a *V* formation and begin a forward motion with arms interlocked in front of the ball carrier before the ball was snapped. The effect was to have a "flying wedge" strike at the opponents before the ball carrier could be reached, often with devastating effect.

The sport continued to attract negative attention from the press, clergy, and some college faculty and administrators.[13] Injuries mounted,

---

12 A well-played game by Yale and Princeton in 1885 and a severe improvement of play helped football gain a greater "public esteem." Weyand, *American Football, Its History and Development*, 28.

13 Harvard President Eliot, in his report delivered in 1893, denounced football as a game coached by young men intent on winning at all costs. He complained that the sport produced "powerful animals with diluted intellects." He feared the impression that colleges were becoming "places of mere physical sport and not an intellectual training." Nevertheless, Eliot's views were not in the majority. College football was drawing large crowds and significant receipts for colleges. In 1887, the Harvard-Yale game, won by national champion Yale, attracted a crowd of some twenty-four thousand people.

and the rules committee was forced to act.[14] In 1894, the "flying wedge" or mass momentum plays were abolished—well, almost. Although the rule did prohibit the "flying wedge," there was an exception carved out permitting up to three players to go in forward motion and provide interference for the ball carrier.[15] The new rules would immediately result in ingenious coaches installing the "tackle back" or the practice of shifting large offensive tackles into the backfield to provide more effective motion and interference for the ball carrier.

Ultimately, the rule changes enacted in 1894 would not prove enough to stem the violent nature of the game nor the criticism that accompanied it. Players would continue to fight, and ball carriers would be pushed, pulled, and even catapulted ahead, sometimes by straps sewn into their uniforms. Players were in many cases seriously injured and in some cases killed. Notable and tragic cases would mount. In 1905, college football resulted in nineteen deaths.[16] College football's response to this crisis is more fully explored in Chapter 8. A skillful diplomacy by Walter Camp and others, together with more significant rules changes, would rescue the game, but not without a close call and much debate.

---

14   The federal government abolished the Army-Navy game in 1894, bowing to mounting public pressure. Ibid., 59.

15   The Intercollegiate Rules Association was disbanded in 1893, and in the vacuum, the big four—Harvard, Princeton, Pennsylvania, and Yale—formed a rules committee that adopted the 1894 changes.

16   Brooks, *Forward Pass*, 14.

—— Chapter Three ——

Leominster and Fitchburg at the Nineteenth Century's Close

As the nineteenth century drew to a close, Leominster was a small but vibrant town, which aptly reflected a growing industrial nation that still clung to some of its agricultural foundation. The town had three banks to help finance its commerce, which included sixteen comb manufacturers, most of which also produced hairpins, other goods from horn, and novelties. A few of those companies, Tilton & Cook, Union Manufacturing, and E.B. Kingman & Co., although now closed, are still familiar today.[17]

---

17 The years 1895–1900 marked a transition away from the use of horn in the manufacture of combs and other goods. E.B. Kingman Co. was one manufacturer that introduced a high-grade line of celluloid products. In 1898, Bernard Doyle, who noted the steady decrease in the supply of horn and the rise of celluloid, investigated a new compound, pyroxylin plastic, which became the impetus to join Alexander S. Paton of Leominster, Ludwig Stross of New York, and Paul Rie of Paris, in forming a large concern known as the Viscoloid Company. Only a few of the sixty-two buildings occupying forty acres of what was the Viscoloid Company remain on Lancaster Street at the intersection of Viscoloid Avenue.

Local business of the 1890s was quite diverse. The town's sole newspaper, the *Leominster Enterprise,* provided an advertising medium for dressmakers, confectioners, grocers, and manufacturers of jewelry, paper boxes, buttons, piano-forte cases, boots and shoes, and at least one cigar maker. Leominster industry famously included the F.A. Whitney Carriage Company, W.S. Reed Toy Company, and the Hudson Apple Parer Company, all prominent in their fields and makers of products avidly collected today.

Mixed in this explosion of industrial expansion was a measure of agricultural production. Local farms still provided a fair amount of the local food supply and fueled part of a transportation system that didn't yet include the automobile. In 1894, the town possessed eight boarding and feed stables and six blacksmiths for its four-legged transportation stock. Agriculture was supported by five grain-and-feed stores, a grist mill, manufacturers of farming implements, and five hay-and-straw dealers. As many as seven farms sold fresh butter and eggs, and five farmers advertised themselves as cucumber growers, including George Kendall, whose prominent greenhouses on North Main Street would earn him the title "cucumber king."[18]

Leisure and the finer things in life were not lost among local wares. A gent could purchase a fashionable derby at Shapley Brothers and enjoy a fine cigar at E. Thomson's Billiard Hall located in the Sawtelle Block on Monument Square. Young people and adults alike could purchase a bicycle from J.H. Wentworth on Mechanic Street.

Electricity had brought improvement and change. Leominster Electric Light and Power Co. had begun the task of bringing electric lights to much of the town. Electricity also powered the trolley cars that could convey businessmen or shoppers to Fitchburg.

The 1890 federal census recorded a Leominster population of 7,269. By contrast, Fitchburg boasted a count of some 22,037. Fitchburg was a mecca of industry. Leading producers of paper, worsted wool, and machinery anchored the local economic base. Fitchburg Paper Company, Crocker Burbank Company, Putnam Machine Company, and Simonds Saw & Steel had reputations and customer bases that extended throughout the nation. The breathtaking

---

Doyle, *Comb Making in America,* 114.
18   *Leominster Directory,* 1893–1894, 50, 103.

growth and advances provided the citizens of Fitchburg an opportunity to encourage benevolence and cultural advances that properly befit a center of commerce and economic importance. The inhabitants of Fitchburg gave proper consideration to the plight of the unfortunate.

The Fitchburg Associated Charities, the new name adopted by the Fitchburg Benevolent Union in 1891, was led for many years by the banker Ebenezer Bailey. Fond of brisk walks and poetry, the energetic Bailey guided efforts to aid the poor for fifty-three years. At age eighty-two, he was still writing poetry and traveling to Lake Whalom to enjoy another lifelong passion, ice skating.[19]

Lake Whalom had become a trolley destination in 1893 when the Fitchburg and Leominster Street Railway Company established a depot at the park. Lake Whalom included facilities for bathing and boating as well as a new toboggan slide. Park-goers could dine at the Whalom Inn or feed the deer, elk, and moose in the animal park. Other attractions included a dance hall and a rustic summer theater that accommodated three thousand patrons paying five cents for general admission and ten cents for reserved seating.[20]

Cultural and charitable gains were made possible by Fitchburg's dramatic growth. Although Leominster's development fell short of Fitchburg's expansion, the town was progressing, and its public institutions reflected that. Leominster was engaged in the construction of a new town hall in 1894. Designed by Boston architects H.H. Richardson, the building would be completed in January, 1895 for a cost of $93,400. The new building sited on the plot occupied by today's city hall included a grand theater with floor and gallery seating for 1,200.[21] Until the town hall was complete, Leominster citizens might take the 7:30 PM electric to Fitchburg and arrive in time for the 8:10 PM performance of the talented reader Miss Gertrude Saunders Jones, whose literary talent was enhanced by sopranos, soloists, and the Russell Orchestra at Fitchburg City Hall on the evening of October

---

19   Kirkpatrick, *The City and the River*, 382–383.
20   *Leominster Enterprise*, October 20, 1894.
21   The "New Town Hall" that replaced the town hall constructed in 1851 was totally destroyed by a fire that raged on the night of December 23, 1909. Rumors persist to this day that the fire was set by an embezzling official to destroy evidence of misdeeds.

24, 1894. Those wishing to stay within the confines of Leominster that evening could take in the play *Finger of Fate or the Death Letter* produced by the Stolen Will Dramatic Company.[22]

The serious business of the nation was never far from mind. Leominster, like many communities its size that had progressed along with the country's industrial expansion, had a stake in America's economy. The economic downturn of 1893 was a topic on the mind of locals who took those matters into consideration during the 1894 congressional election. Leominster was a conservative town, and its newspaper and the majority of its citizens endorsed the Republican platform. Populist congressional candidate Bertram Sparhawk visited town hall in October of 1894, urging Leominster citizens to abandon both Cleveland Democrats and Harrison Republicans. The *Leominster Enterprise* covered the event:

> The speaker cited Rome and all ancient forms of government and told how they "went down," and this country was sure to follow unless another political party came to the rescue. We need harmony. The two great parties are antagonistic. At one time they want Harrison and then they want Cleveland. The masses of the people "go down" because there is a want of good government and they become demoralized and sink to a "low level." People are out of employment and factories are idle. The speaker said he was formerly a Republican and his whole family were Republicans. There should be a new party. No one has any confidence in any party now in power. The speaker said he could see but little difference between the Democrats and Republicans.[23]

Most of the Leominster audience walked out of the hall long before Mr. Sparhawk could finish his lecture. Leominster was not ready to abandon its Republican leanings or endorse the wholesale change represented by a brand-new political party. Nevertheless, manufacturing and novel inventions and improvements were already a part of local

---

22   *Leominster Enterprise*, December 24, 1909.
23   *Leominster Enterprise*, October 20, 1894.

cultures. Leominsters and Fitchburgs, as they sometimes referred to themselves, were also ready to sample new activities and pastimes that would include an evolving, dramatic, and passionate sport, the object of which was to push, pull, force, and batter until a watermelon-shaped leather sphere could be brought across a goal.

—— Chapter Four ——

The 1890s Bring Football
to Leominster and Fitchburg

Football gained a hold on the imagination of the young men and lady spectators of Fitchburg and Leominster as early as 1891. At first a rather informal game, participants included high school boys as well as unenrolled young men of high school and college age. Football and its historic foundation, rugby, had existed on eastern college campuses since 1876 and under the rules of the "old association" (a soccer-style version of the game) for seven years before that.[24] Not all members of the public viewed football as a positive influence in the lives of young men. In 1873, Cornell University President Andrew D. White responded to a request to send the college's football team to Cleveland for a game as follows: "I refuse to let forty boys travel four hundred miles merely to agitate a bag of wind."[25] What appeal did football have to Americans in the late nineteenth century, and how did that manifest itself in Leominster and Fitchburg?

The generation of young men coming of age at the end of the nineteenth century was the first of that epoch who did not face the prospect of war and hostility. The prior decades witnessed conflicts

24   Ibid., xv.
25   Time-Life Books, *This Fabulous Century*, 162.

involving the annexation of territory, slavery, the geographic distribution of political power, and the subjugation of the Native American population. In succession, boys marched off to fight in the Mexican War, the War Between the States, and the Indian fights of the plains. The last generation of the century was steeped in tales of valor and honor by their fathers and grandfathers. The final male representatives of the century, who came of age with America's growing economic power, needed an outlet for the exhibition of masculine prowess. Football, a game that included all of the requirements of warfare—tactics, bravery, and strength—became that outlet.

The bravado of football in the 1890s was not foreign to the ladies either. The *Leominster Enterprise* noted a game with the "Fitchburgs" on Saturday, November 11, 1893 where gents were admitted for twenty-five cents and ladies for free. The same note indicated, "(football) is at flood tide just now and the game this afternoon will doubtless draw a large crowd."[26] The local news sections of the November 29, 1898

---

26   The 1893 game pitting the "Leominsters" and the "Fitchburgs" might qualify as a high school game even though at least some of the participants were not in high school. The game long recognized as the first between the high schoolers on October 20, 1894 was questioned by Fitchburg residents of years past who doubted that it truly was a high school game. The confusion results from the essential fact that high school football of the 1890s was highly informal and not highly regulated by the high schools. Therefore, it was a regular practice that so-called high school teams included non-high school players as well as the converse. The 1949 Thanksgiving program contained an article entitled "A Controversy" that started as follows:
Any discussion of the Leominster-Fitchburg football rivalry very often produces an argument—for the most part friendly— but, usually an argument. The very inception of this series is a controversial issue which Old Father Time in fifty-five, or is it fifty-four years, has never been able to settle. Fitchburg authorities insist that this schoolboy series, one of the oldest in the country, officially started in 1895. Leominster authorities are just as insistent that the first game took place one year earlier—1894. Thus it has been through the years, a relentless controversy, never settled to the complete satisfaction of either party." Leominster High School game program, printed by Leominster Printing Company.

edition of the *Leominster Enterprise* quipped, in addition to noting the upcoming Thanksgiving match between Leominster and Clinton:

> It has always been a custom in the past to admit women for free at the LHS football games; accordingly, the fair sex will be granted the same privilege at the game Thanksgiving morning and any fellow can take along his girl and not drain his purse by paying admittance for two.[27]

One of the earliest football contests played in Leominster pitted the locals against the Lancasters at the old driving park on Friday, November 20, 1891, and the visitors prevailed. The earliest reported Thanksgiving game occurred on Thursday, November 26, 1891.

> The foot-ball game at the park last Thursday between the *married and unmarried boys*, drew a large crowd. Set a dish of dough large enough for three hungry chickens to eat from; then let in five hundred to see them all try for a beakfull, and you can get a good idea of it. However, there was lots of fun.[28]

Fitchburg's young men were also experiencing early football yearnings. On September 11, 1885, the *Fitchburg Sentinel* reported the inclusion of a football game along with baseball and bicycle races at the Odd Fellows Field Day to be held in Worcester on September 16. In 1891,

---

27 On October 29, 1901, the *Leominster Enterprise* announced, "At next Saturday's football game, admission will be charged for ladies as well as their escorts. The boys have found it necessary in order to make ends meet." Those who chose not to pay any gate at all and viewed the contest from outside the fence or rope were called "deadheads." That practice was especially difficult in the years before Doyle Field when Leominster played its home games behind the high school on West Street (later Carter Junior High) from 1918–1930. During those years, Fitchburg refused to play any Thanksgiving game in Leominster, preferring to utilize the greatly superior Crocker Field.

28 *Leominster Enterprise*, November 28, 1891.

the *Sentinel's* high school notes section reported that Mr. Chapin put an end to the practice of kicking the football in the streets near the high school building on account of liability for broken windows. The newspaper remarked, "What a pity it is that there is not a field large enough near the school which could be used for football, baseball and other games."[29] A lack of adequate field plagued Fitchburg boys in 1892 as well. "The high school boys were obliged to play their football game on Garfield's 'Mountain House Field' on account of the discourtesy of the lessee of 'Rye Field.'" Despite the accommodations, the game was played, and Fosdick's side beat Park's side 30–14.[30]

One *Leominster Enterprise* report from 1893 revealed the editor's misgivings about the game of "foot-ball" when the local team did not fare well.

> Foot-ball still flourishes. The example of Harvard and Yale seems to have spread over the country. Last Saturday, the Leominsters enjoyed a most rousing defeat, but if the Sentinel is authority, they are not discouraged. The way we look at it, after a man has been knocked down and walked over and stamped on, he ought to be discouraged if he is intending to ever be. It is possible that this is a wonderfully scientific game, but we are not anxious to learn that science.[31]

Despite the dour view pervading that newspaper item, the youth of Leominster and Fitchburg did vigorously and enthusiastically seek to emulate the popular intercollegiate football programs. By 1894, college football had grown sufficiently in popularity to produce storied rivalries, national champions, and star-powered all-American teams.[32]

"In those infant days of college football, students decked out in

---

29   *Fitchburg Sentinel*, November 18, 1891.
30   *Fitchburg Sentinel*, October 22, 1892.
31   *Leominster Enterprise*, November 15, 1893.
32   Walter Camp and Casper Whitney selected the nation's first "All-American" team in 1889. Honorees included end Amos Alonzo Stagg of Yale, who would become one of college football's most legendary coaches and innovators, as well as Princeton's back Edgar Allen Poe, a direct descendant of the author and namesake.

coats, vests, ties, and bowlers crowded the boundary lines of the grassy malls or dirt fields where the games were staged. Clutching and waving handmade pennants, they devised spontaneous cheers to urge their compatriots to victory. From the very beginning, college football was as much—perhaps more—of a contest for its fans than its players."[33]

---

33   Excerpt is © Whittingham, Richard. *Rites of Autumn—The Story of College Football,* New York: The Free Press, 2001, xii.

—— Chapter Five ——

The First Game between Rivals, October 20, 1894?

For at least the past forty years, October 20, 1894 has been considered the date when Leominster and Fitchburg High Schools first met on the gridiron. While the story of that meeting is compelling, it is by no means certain that the 1894 game can be considered conclusively as "the game" that initiated the historic series. As noted in the previous chapter, high school football of the nineteenth century was highly informal and did not entail any significant regulation by high school administrators. It was not uncommon for so called "high school" squads to include players of questionable eligibility, players not enrolled in school. Early newspaper accounts of high school games frequently include either express complaints or hints as to player eligibility.[34]

It is clear that a high school football team was formed in Leominster during the autumn of 1893. On September 23 of that year, the *Leominster Enterprise* reported, "And now the Leominster High School

---

34 The September 30, 1898 edition of the *Leominster Enterprise* contained a note that "The High boys have chosen Sidney E. Bell, Manager of what they desire to make a *strictly* high school football team." (emphasis added)

boys are making great preparations for a successful college life. They have organized a foot-ball team."

The brief entry establishes a great deal in few words. High school boys were intent on attaining the star power already a feature of college programs that had garnered national prominence. Additionally, the two sentences indicate and emphasize that "they," the high school boys, had organized the team. On Wednesday, September 13, 1893, teams from Leominster and Fitchburg played a football game during the Leominster Cattle Show and Fair. The *Fitchburg Sentinel* reported the game the following day, which the Leominster eleven won 8–6. The newspaper account included the names of the players. Two of the listed names, Gane and Cawthorne, were members of the Leominster High School team of 1894. Four additional names listed—England, Mahan, Hathaway, and Dyer—played as high school alumni of Leominster against the Leominster High School eleven on Thanksgiving Day of 1894. On November 4 of that same autumn, the *Leominster Enterprise* announced that:

> The football game of the season will be played at the Leominster Driving Park, Saturday afternoon at 3 o'clock; between the Fitchburgs and Leominsters. Admission, gents 25 cents; ladies free. Much interest is taken in football games this season. It is at flood tide just now and the game this afternoon will doubtless draw a large crowd.[35]

There are other hints as to the informal nature of high school football during the 1890s; not only did questions arise as to eligibility of players, but even the ownership of the "football suits" gave rise to a certain amount of controversy when competing claims of the school and the players themselves had to be sorted out.

During the autumn of 1894, high school football teams were organized in Leominster and Fitchburg. It was only natural that these squads would face each other—again. However destined the football match was, details of the meeting remained to be worked out. There

---

35 Judging by the 1893 game report carried in the *Leominster Enterprise* and set out in the prior chapter—Fitchburg was dominant.

were no school administrators or athletic directors to set schedules. The games were negotiated by team managers who themselves were high school students. Managers were dispatched like diplomats with credentials and the instructions necessary to agree on a game.

On Tuesday, September 25, 1894, the *Fitchburg Sentinel* carried an item in its "school notes" section: "The team … has received a challenge from Leominster High School to play a football game at Leominster Saturday afternoon." The challenge was accepted, and on the following Thursday, the *Fitchburg Sentinel* reported the Fitchburg football team planned to "go down on the 1 PM electric from the American House" on Saturday, September 29. For reasons unknown, Leominster postponed the game.

Undeterred, the teams rescheduled their football game for Friday, October 5; however, once again, Leominster postponed the meeting. The report of the second postponement in the *Fitchburg Sentinel* was nothing less than a complete indictment of Leominster's honor.

> The game which was to have been played with Leominster this afternoon was again postponed by Leominster, as they play Murdock School tomorrow. The team has become disgusted with this kind of treatment by Leominster and probably will not play them at all. Fitchburg has been greatly strengthened this week and Leominster is undoubtedly afraid of them.[36]

No self-respecting group of high school football warriors could let those words echo without response. Arrangements were made to conduct a summit between respective delegations from both teams. Leominster sent its manager and team captain to Fitchburg on Tuesday, October 16, 1894, and it was agreed that Fitchburg would travel to Leominster for a game on Saturday, October 20 at 3:00 PM. This time, the trolley from Fitchburg did carry its high school football players to Leominster's driving park for the much-anticipated gridiron meeting. For reasons not wholly understood, the fading light of that October afternoon, and

---

36   *Fitchburg Sentinel*, October 5, 1894.

not the prior or succeeding years, fixed in history that game as the first between two traditional foes in one of the oldest rivalries in football.

Teamwork has been heralded as a football essential from the infancy of the sport. In the last minutes of daylight, the Leominsters efficiently dispatched the Fitchburg squad with an impressive display of team play. Not unexpectedly, the press from each town recorded a different perspective on the game's outcome. On one point, there was not disagreement. The *Fitchburg Sentinel* reported on Monday, October 22, 1894, "The Leominsters won the game by their fine team work, the best a local team ever showed on their grounds." An equal appreciation of the Leominsters' performance was recorded in the host town's newspaper. The *Leominster Enterprise* of Saturday, October 27 concluded, "The Leominster team played a sharp, quick game and their interference was impregnable … It was the best exhibition of team work ever given by a Leominster team …"[37]

Witnesses to these early competitions came away impressed by selfless and physical contributions of the supporting cast. The work of the halfbacks of the 1890s was that of ground gainers, the sustainers of an offense that did not include the forward pass. Walter Camp noted, "such work calls for dash and fire—that ability to suddenly concentrate all the bodily energy into an effort that must make way through anything."[38] "Dash and fire" certainly attracted the crowd's focus and admiration, but no halfback, regardless of skill and size, makes his way through "anything" without well-placed, well-timed interference by teammates willing to hold up their end, sometimes literally, for the greater good. One of those teammates providing a solid wall or blocks for the running backs was Mark O'Toole. Growing up as the "man of the house" with a widowed mother and four younger sisters must have taught O'Toole a little something about sacrifice and teamwork. These football warriors of antiquity accepted a division of tasks and duties and sought valor from the field with no less vigor than a military force.

Leominster's left halfback, Henry Foster, was the most prolific scorer that October afternoon, notching four touchdowns and accounting for sixteen of the forty points the host team posted. Fitchburg's efforts did not yield a single point. The Dewes brothers, Arthur and Joseph,

---

37   *Leominster Enterprise*, October 27, 1894.
38   Camp, *American Football,* 93.

combined to score four goals, or try after touchdowns, for a total of eight points. Arthur, the quarterback, booted three goals through the uprights, and Joseph, the fullback, added the fourth. The balance of scoring, sixteen points, resulted from four additional touchdowns. Arthur Kittredge, the right halfback, scored two, and both of the ends, Edward Cawthorne on the right side and Louis Gane his opposite, each added an additional touchdown.

Contemporary newspaper accounts were predictably slanted. Given the laxity of oversight pervading high school football of the Gay Nineties, it is not surprising that issues of player age and eligibility were woven into explanations of game outcome. The *Fitchburg Sentinel* noted that all but Leominster's two tackles were veteran players. Any ambiguity as to the meaning of the term "veteran" was resolved by the next sentence. "Much more credit is due FHS team who, instead of *challenging* players and refusing to play unless they were withdrawn, displayed their genuine sportsmanlike spirit by going in and playing for all they were worth … They showed that it would have been a fairly equal game if they had as much experience as the opponents."[39] Despite a relative lack of experience, Fitchburg's left end Clifford Godbeer's tackling was outstanding. Young Godbeer roamed the field as rugged as the granite in his father's quarry, felling Leominster's ball carriers with all the energy he could muster.

The *Leominster Enterprise* validated the superior experience of its hometown boys and maintained the "essential equity" of the competition. "On the Leominster side though they are *not to* be considered as a school team it is to be said that they are in the *same class* as the high school teams." (emphasis added) The Leominster newspaper complimented the visitors. "They showed that they were not the kind to back down, and lined up in good style; their contention, however, that is could in no way be considered a match game between two schools is good and valid …"

The Leominster team was led that day by a coach, E.J. Cutter, who was a medical doctor. Dr. Cutter lived and maintained his practice on Pearl Street, a short walk to Leominster's Field High School. The passing years have obscured much about Coach Cutter. To be sure, his position was unpaid, and a love of the game supplied the necessary motivation.

---

39   *Fitchburg Sentinel*, October 22, 1894.

Dr. Cutter likely possessed an inquisitive nature that invited challenge. During the summer and autumn of 1890, the doctor spent five months in Europe for the purpose of conducting "a special study of the eye and ear." A "local note" in the *Leominster Enterprise* welcomed him home. "All will be rejoiced to see the Dr. in his place once more."[40]

Leominster's players entered the foray with a coach that undoubtedly had a presence. During a doctor's visit in November of 1891, his hitched team was spooked by a dog's howl when the carriage shifted and its wheel backed into the unfortunate hound. The resulting chain of events caused the carriage to topple, a "demoralization" of one of its wheels and a horse that dashed away "leaving the whole of his attachments at a stone post…" The good doctor, once alerted, "spoke to him (the horse) … the animal stopped short and stood quietly until his master approached."[41]

Sadly, Dr. Cutter would meet an early death, succumbing to a stroke at age forty-five. However, that autumn, and in particular the Saturday that the Fitchburgs came calling, Dr. Cutter accompanied his boys to the driving park for a fateful football match. His charges did not disappoint.[42]

That afternoon and the Leominster team's dominant performance served notice that the smaller community came to play. Nothing between the high schools would ever be quite the same. The gridiron would provide each community a venue, a proving ground for its young men to earn a measure of respect as comrades in battle. The *Leominster Enterprise* admitted had Fitchburg been of equal experience, the Leominsters would have been "seriously inconvenienced … When Fitchburg has had that, they will show the Leominster team a thing or two."[43]

The die was cast and the competition inaugurated. A rivalry was forged that has endured more than eleven decades of change that, by measure of technological advance, surpasses the scientific achievement of the entire span of recorded history before that game. The rivalry would seep into the fabric of both towns, and through the years, folks

---

40   *Leominster Enterprise*, November 15, 1890.
41   *Leominster Enterprise*, November 21, 1891.
42   *Leominster Enterprise*, November 21, 1891.
43   *Leominster Enterprise*, October 27, 1894.

would debate just how much of that rivalry spilled over into a simmering cauldron of competition that extended far beyond the football field. No answer is necessary; the debate itself is proof enough.

It is hard to imagine what existed before rivalries emerged. What would the Harvard football team be without Yale? What would excite the cadets of the United States Military Academy if there was never a United States Naval Academy team? Football, more than any sport, creates and sustains rivalry. It is the very essence and texture of the game. Traditional competition is enhanced by physical danger, cunning, and sacrifice for the principle of team. A team-first attitude has and will continue to produce rivals.

Chapter Six

The Rivalry Gains Its Footing

"We Read everyday or so such a statement as this: 'The LHS will play the Lancaster High School boys at the park Saturday,' or 'Our home town team played a splendid game and won.' Would it not be well to vary this once in a while and see how the boys rank in an intellectual contest? We are told football is most excellent for discipline. Very good, *perhaps* it is. Make good the boasting by showing what the boys are intellectually. We shall be most pleased to hear."

J.D. Miller, Editor and Publisher, *Leominster Enterprise,* November 23, 1895

People were still getting used to the football craze in 1895. The game had its doubters. Questions continued over a growing number of violent injuries. Editor Miller's commentary was shared by a number of people who openly wondered whether this game was changing the focus in high school and universities from academics to athletics. Novel activities that gain popular heights, especially those that appeal to youth, will always raise questions with the more mature segment of society. Football was no exception.

Football's growing popularity during the last years of the 1890s was fueled by an intense interest in college football programs and rivalries already firmly established. In November of 1895, the *Leominster Enterprise* reported, "The football craze seems to be of no small proportions, not only in Leominster but also in all parts of the country. It is a first-class game for all who like it." By 1895, the tradition of Harvard and Yale football was already a national sensation. Clifford Godbeer traveled to Springfield, Massachusetts with his older brother John in November of 1894 to watch a football match between Harvard and Yale. The trip was enough of an event to be carried in the West Fitchburg news section of the *Fitchburg Sentinel* on November 24, 1894. The Godbeers witnessed Yale and its five first-team all-Americans prevail over Harvard in that installment of their intense rivalry.[44]

Yale and Pennsylvania were the college football powers of 1895. Pennsylvania had a perfect 14–0 record in 1895, outscoring its opponents an astounding 480–24. The vanquished included Harvard, Cornell, Brown, Pennsylvania State, Lafayette, Virginia, Carlisle, Lehigh, Bucknel, Swarthmore, Franklin, and Marshall. Yale was undefeated that same year, achieving thirteen victories and two ties, while outscoring its opponents an impressive 318–38. Yale was victorious over Princeton, Brown, Carlisle, Army, Dartmouth (twice), Williams, Amherst, Union, Trinity, and a number of club teams. Yale's two ties were with the Boston Athletic Club and Brown, having faced the latter twice that year. Yale's match with Princeton drew a great deal of attention in that year. Yale and Harvard did not meet that season, and Princeton was a common opponent that provided a comparative measure of the two traditional rivals. "The great event of interest in foot-ball is the Yale-Princeton game to be played in New York Nov. 23d. Princeton has already beaten Harvard and it is expected that this game will throw much light on the comparative merits of Yale and Harvard. It will also show whether Yale is gaining or losing in athletic matters. Lovers of football for these reasons will watch the game with great interest."[45]

Pennsylvania's rise to college football prominence was a rather recent occurrence. "Until three years ago, when the University of Pennsylvania forged into the front rank, these three colleges (Harvard, Yale, and Princeton) shared about all the trophies there were. Numbers

---

44 *Fitchburg Sentinel*, November 24, 1894.
45 *Leominster Enterprise*, November 23, 1895.

are now telling, and colleges with more students than Princeton, for instance, are asserting their athletic rights. This is why Harvard and Yale find instead of having but one or two 'big' games a year, they have a sharp game almost each week."[46]

While Pennsylvania and Yale were dominating the gridiron in 1895, high school football players in Fitchburg and Leominster were eager to emulate their college counterparts. At least some of the high schoolers' elders were not as keen for the gridiron. It is tantalizing conjecture as to what was discussed at a lecture advertised in the *Leominster Enterprise* on Saturday, November 16, 1895, "After the Football What?' is the subject to be discussed in the chapel of the Orthodox [sic] Congressional Church tomorrow evening at 6:30 by Principal Meserve and sub-master Wright of the High School, C.H. Rice, J.D. Miller and Dr. Scott all are cordially invited." The young men and others who enjoyed football were undeterred. As the Leominsters and Fitchburgs met in 1895, neither the adherents of football nor those with questions could imagine that this second game between the schools (assuming you accept the historical tradition of 1894 as the first game) would serve as early traction for one of the oldest football rivalries in America. Fitchburg defeated Leominster in 1895 by a score of 14–6.

Leominster and Fitchburg were commencing a conflict, most often friendly, that continues until today. Ironically, the autumn of 1895 witnessed a reconciliation of a far more embittered and serious conflict. On September 8, the *Leominster Enterprise* reported that the Stevens Post of the Grand Army of the Republic of Leominster had the honor of being the first G.A.R. Post to arrive on a "peaceful invasion of the south" for an encampment of veterans from both sides of the conflict between the states in Louisville, Kentucky. The Leominster Civil War Veterans visited the Cave Hill Cemetery, "where so many faithful followers of both sides lie buried."[47] Reports from the encampment noted the most gracious hospitality of the southern host city.

---

46   *Boston Journal,* November 13, 1895.

47   Sadly, the *Leominster Enterprise* contained an item the following week, "In Louisville, the Grand Army of the Republic and fraternity at wholesale. In South Carolina, a convention to deprive the Negro of his right to vote. Truly this is a great world and there are several people in it." *Leominster Enterprise,* September 14, 1895.

Fortunately, the conflicts of 1895 were confined to the football field. Despite the loss to Fitchburg, the 1895 season included two victories against Clinton High by scores of 14–0 and 42–0. The boys bested Ayer High School 8–4 and met Gardner High twice, beating the Chair City eleven 10–4 in their second meeting. The first game with Gardner ended in a scoreless tie. "Neither side made a single point, but there was some tall squabbling for a victory."[48]

Leominster would meet Fitchburg on the football field seven more times in the nineteenth century, twice per season in the years 1897–1899. Fitchburg, whether owing to its much larger population or otherwise, was dominant. The scores were as follows:

1896	Fitchburg 18, Leominster 0
1897	Fitchburg 4, Leominster 0
1897	Fitchburg 8, Leominster 0
1898	Leominster 5, Fitchburg 0
1898	Fitchburg 5, Leominster 0
1899	Fitchburg 10, Leominster 0
1899	Tie 0–0

If the nineteenth century crowds enjoyed defense, they apparently had their fill. The loser of all nine contests played in the nineteenth century did not score a single point, except when Leominster scored six in the 1895 loss to Fitchburg. In the seven contests played between 1896 and 1899, Leominster managed a total of but five points! Leominster's only points in those four years came on a single touchdown (point value: five), scored in the first meeting between the schools in 1898.

Prior to the call of young men to the high school gridiron in the autumn of 1898, the nation beckoned America's young men for a far more serious duty. In April that year, Congress authorized a fighting force of two hundred thousand to respond to tensions with Spain over its conduct in governing Cuba and the dramatic explosion and sinking of the USS Maine in Havana's harbor. Some 223,000 young men volunteered for service, including Mark O'Toole, whose first volunteer effort occurred four years earlier as a member of Leominster

---

48   *Leominster Enterprise,* October 23, 1895.

High School's football team. O'Toole entered active service on May 6, 1898 as a private in Company D of the Sixth Massachusetts Regiment amidst a panic that gripped the Atlantic seaboard when the hostile Spanish fleet left the Cape Verde Islands for location unknown. The Spanish empire was reduced that summer by America's emerging military power in 105 days, between May 1 and August 13. Captain O'Toole, who was quickly promoted, was deployed on an expedition of the Puerto Rican coast. At the end of hostilities, the men of the Sixth Massachusetts Regiment found themselves stranded in the Town of Utuado, subsisting on hard tack and tomato soup. Finally, Massachusetts Governor Wolcott interceded with President McKinley on their behalf and the men were returned to the United States.[49]

International hostilities abated, and as autumn approached, the residents of Fitchburg and Leominster could turn their attention to leisure and sport. Clifford Godbeer, who played so effectively for Fitchburg High School in 1894, never graduated high school. Godbeer, who chose not to follow his father as a stone mason, was working for the Fitchburg Railroad as a clerk in the engineering office in 1898. Godbeer's interest in sport would continue. Clifford and his older brother John participated in YMCA games held in Fitchburg during September of 1898. Each brother entered the one hundred-yard dash, broad jump, and shot-put events.

Nevertheless, football got a less-than-confident start at Fitchburg High School that year. The thought of fielding a team took hold only after the relative ineptitude of the usual competition was assessed. The FHS 1899 yearbook summed up the '98 season:

> After about one month's practice, the outlook being somewhat discouraging, it was agreed that disbandment would be best for the team. During October the idea of football was a lost chord in the high school, but as other teams appeared as weak as ours, and showed of it in their games, a longing soon arose in the school for a good strong game with the pigskins. Practice started again in the last week of October.

---

49   Edwards, *The '98 Campaign of the 6th Massachusetts U.S.V.*, 181–182.

Leominster High's 1898 season started with greater promise. In those days, the high school football season was generally confined to the bright blue skies of October and November's gray horizons, culminating with a contest on Thanksgiving Day. With their manager chosen, the "enthusiastic" Leominsters began practicing on Houghton Hill, modern-day Grove Avenue. Apparently, the boys' enthusiasm was met with the support of Leominster's businessmen as "(t)he prominent men of the Town ... respond(ed) generously to the appeal of the LHS Football Team for money."[50] The football team's support might have been partially rooted in a controversy over the ownership of the football suits that season. Thursday, September 28, 1898, the *Fitchburg Sentinel* carried an item titled, "Who Owns The Football Suits." The story continued, "(t)here is a tempest in a teapot over football matters at the high school." A fellow named Edward F. Killelea, who was forming a football team at the beginning of the school term, not strictly confined to high school boys, had possession of the uniforms belonging to the first Leominster Football Team. The suits had been handed down player to player and the issue arose in 1898 as to whether the "suits" were loaned or given to the high school boys. Killelea maintained the football suits were his property after making a bargain with the former owner. Nevertheless, Principal Mason "took a hand in the matter as the chief of police was asked to get the suits." Interestingly, the very next day, the *Fitchburg Sentinel* carried a notice by Fitchburg High's team manager requesting a return of all "football material," given that the Fitchburg High School season was in doubt of proceeding. Not to be outdone, Fitchburg's popular Iver Johnson Store placed an advertisement in the *Fitchburg Sentinel* for football pants a week later.[51]

Once practice was underway, the Leominster High team came down "severely crippled ... by the loss of several of their best men. Metcalf, who was intending to play left guard, is unable to play, and Perry, is unable to play because of a bicycle accident. Hadley, the star half back cannot leave work and cannot play at all this season, and to cap the climax, Friday evening, while practicing at the Old Common, Henry McCarthy, the full back, fell on a broken bottle and cut a deep gash in his arm which will prevent him from being in the lineup for

---

50   *Leominster Enterprise*, October 14, 1898.
51   *Fitchburg Sentinel*, October 5, 1898.

several weeks."[52] The injuries would heal sufficiently for the *Leominster Enterprise* to remark on Saturday, October 15, 1898, "with some of the cripples in shape they will make a better showing at Gardner next week then they did at Ashburnham." The foe at Ashburnham was a larger, powerful opponent, Cushing Academy. The team traveled to Ashburnham for its thrashing in Pierce's barge, a large horse-drawn carriage. In those days, Josiah Pierce maintained a livery stable on the corner of Main and Mechanic Streets, the present-day site of Bank of America.

Despite the initial indifference by Fitchburg High School in the establishment of a team that season, Leominster's manager, Sidney Bell, arranged for a game to be played in Leominster on October 14. The *Fitchburg Sentinel* reported, "The game is being arranged to oblige the Leominster High School, consequently it has been agreed that none of the teachers there will play with that team." The debate over the nature and makeup of teams continued.

The game was postponed, and the two squads would not face each other in October. Fitchburg's football campaign would not get off the ground until November, and Leominster was enjoying precious little success in the first month of the 1898 season. On October 26, Gardner High dominated Leominster by a score of 21–0. The following Saturday, October 29, Leominster lost to Murdock High School 16–0. That loss was exacerbated by the view that Murdock was a weak team. The Leominster section of the *Fitchburg Sentinel* noted, "Football seems to be a lost art with the high school team." The news concluded with the following: "A few public spirited citizens who have the fair name of Leominster at heart are seriously considering the idea of offering a cash prize to the team if it scores in any game this season."

Perhaps the thinly veiled insult, even without the cash, was enough. Leominster faced Fitchburg for the first time that season on Friday, November 4, and for the first time scored both points and victory. The game was played at Leominster's driving park. The winning and only score came when Leominster's left tackle, Knowlton, picked up a fumble and dashed forty yards for a touchdown. In spite of their loss, Fitchburg came away satisfied with their first effort and game experience that season. The teams would face each other again that

---

52 *Leominster Enterprise*, September 30, 1898.

season, but before that contest, Leominster had a second chance at Murdock High on Saturday, November 12.

The Leominsters missed their train connection to Winchendon, the home of Murdock High School. Once again, the team was traveling by horse-drawn conveyance, which arrived in Winchendon late. The team, numb from the cold ride, played one-half of the football game that the remaining daylight permitted. In those twenty minutes of play, Murdock was again victorious over Leominster 11–0. Between Leominster games, the Fitchburg contingent tied what they deemed a "strong" Murdock team on November 9 and defeated Clinton High School on November 11.

On November 16, Fitchburg got its second chance at Leominster on their home turf, the Circle Street grounds. Buried in the long history of this rivalry is this contest, which has to contend as one of the most controversial of the series. The teams played each other scoreless until very late in the game. With just a little more than one minute left, Leominster punted away to Fitchburg's Dillon, who fielded the punt and began his runback. The home crowd could not contain its excitement, and several of them ran onto the field of play, providing significant interference, which in the judgment of the game official permitted Dillon's fifty-five-yard scamper for a touchdown. The referee, Mr. Lincoln, called the touchdown back, seeking to return the ball to midfield with just a minute of play remaining. Fitchburg's Captain Kirby refused to accept the penalty and, as far as the Fitchburgs were concerned, including their newspaper, the game was won 5–0. Lost in the "objectivity" of the *Fitchburg Sentinel's* reporting was the fact that Lincoln, judging the chaos of the scene, declared the game over, *and more importantly, tied* 0–0! Thus, for the past 110 years, the *Fitchburg Sentinel* has continued to record the game as a Fitchburg victory, despite the judgment of the referee who officiated the game.[53]

The rest of the 1898 season was anti-climatic. Leominster defeated Clinton High School on November 24, Thanksgiving Day, by a score of 15–0. Fitchburg High played its final game of the season at Gardner on November 18, losing by a score of 22–0. Apparently, still buoyed by their "victory" over Leominster, the Fitchburg team returned from

---

53   *Fitchburg Sentinel*, November 17, 1898.

Gardner by train, "in a merry mood, humming, 'There's a red light on the track for Boozer Brown.'"[54]

Whatever the relative merits of "Boozer Brown," the 1898 season, which started with promise for Leominster and discouragement for Fitchburg, produced mediocrity for both teams. Despite a marked lack of success on the part of the "old-time rivals," it is quite clear that games against each other were rapidly taking on new dynamics.

The games of 1898 were building blocks in the architecture of what was fastly becoming competition of a very special nature.

---

54 Fitchburg High School Yearbook for Academic Year 1898–1899.

Leominster High School team of 1894: Dr. E.J. Cutter, coach, is standing far left, and Mark L. O'Toole is seated in the second row, far left.

Fitchburg High School team of 1894.

Unidentified Leominster nineteenth-century football player.

Leominster football player Louis Richardson, circa 1891. Richardson played for Phillips Exeter Academy.

Leominster player Joseph Goodhue posing at the Leominster Driving Park, venue for early Leominster football games (now the upper portion of Doyle Field), circa 1896.

Mark L. O'Toole, a member of the Leominster High School football team of 1894, pictured in his uniform as a Spanish-American War veteran.

Fitchburg High School players from the early twentieth century at the Circle Street grounds, future site of Crocker Field.

Early football action at Crocker Field.

Early football action at Crocker Field.

Early football action at Crocker Field.

Unidentified Leominster High School football player of 1906.

A nineteenth-century trolley car in front of Leominster's town hall, an example of the conveyance football players would have traveled on between Leominster and Fitchburg. The town hall pictured was completed in 1895 but was later destroyed by fire on December 23, 1909.

1900 Leominster High School squad, which did not face Fitchburg High School as a result of the later team suspending its season for poor grades.

Student sketch from 1902 Fitchburg High School Yearbook.

Sketch by student John Vaillant from the 1908 Fitchburg High School Yearbook.

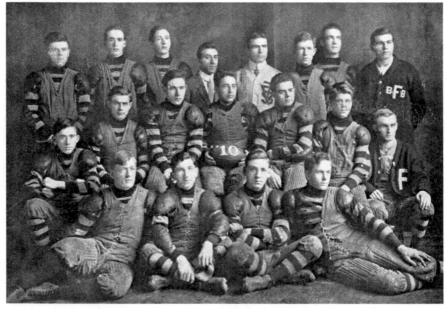

1910 Fitchburg High School team; Clarence Amiott, who would become a coaching legend at his alma mater, is holding the football.

Coach Clarence Amiott.

Fitchburg High School 1911 team at Fitchburg's Circle Street grounds, future site of Crocker Field.

1920s Fitchburg High School team with Crocker Field House in the background.

Modern photograph of the museum room at the Crocker Field House.

Action photo from Crocker Field.

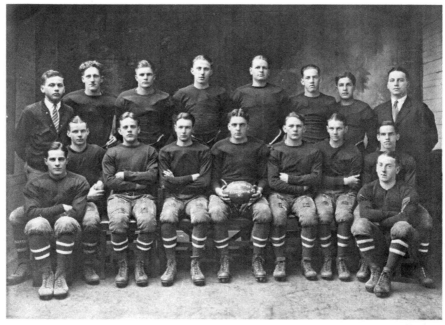

1925 Leominster High School team—victors over Fitchburg for the first time since 1912.

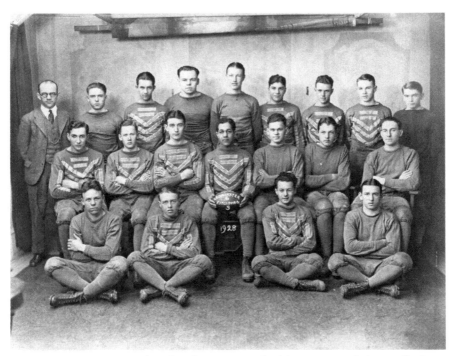

1928 Leominster High School team, coached by Raymond Comerford.

1930 Leominster High School team—the last squad to be coached by Raymond Comerford before his tragic drowning death in August 1931.

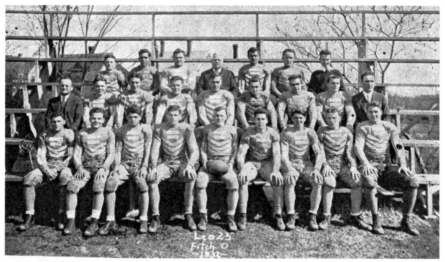

Undefeated Leominster High School team of 1932.

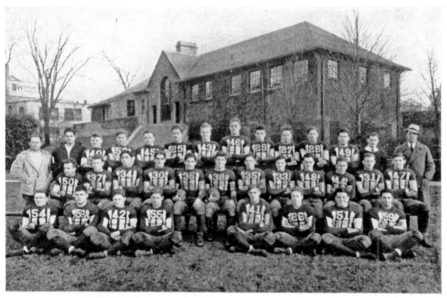

Undefeated Fitchburg High School team of 1933, the only year in the rivalry in which both teams met on Thanksgiving while undefeated.

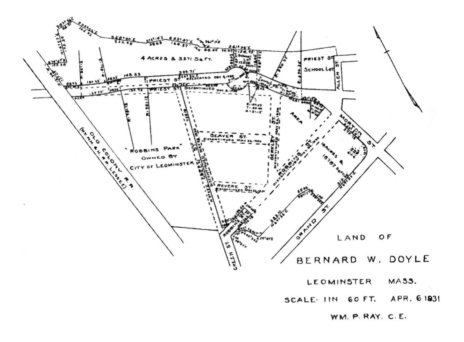

LAND OF

BERNARD W. DOYLE

LEOMINSTER   MASS.

SCALE· 1IN 60 FT.   APR. 6 1931

WM. P. RAY. C.E.

Plan of land for proposed Doyle Field showing streets needing to be discontinued for construction.

Undeveloped Doyle Field at the intersection of Revere and Green Streets.

Former mayor and donor Bernard Doyle speaks at the dedication of Doyle Field on October 10, 1931.

FOOTBALL

FITCHBURG

– VS –

LEOMINSTER

THANKSGIVING DAY

DOYLE FIELD   « »   LEOMINSTER, MASS.

PRICE 10 CENTS

Program of the 1931 Thanksgiving Day game, the first Leominster-Fitchburg game to be held at Doyle Field.

Dorothy (Pierce) Ricker cheers for Leominster High School's undefeated team of 1932.

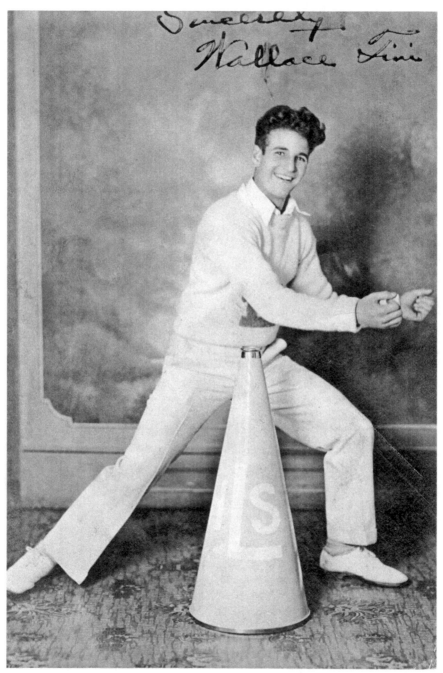

Wallace Fini cheers for Leominster High School in 1932.

Rick Cavaioli, center for the undefeated 1932 Leominster High School football team.

Coach Charles Broderick, the longest-tenured Leominster High School coach—thirty-four seasons—from 1931 to 1964.

The legendary Ronnie Cahill, who was a triple threat at Leominster High School in 1931, 1932, and 1933. Cahill played one season for the Chicago Cardinals of the National Football League in 1943.

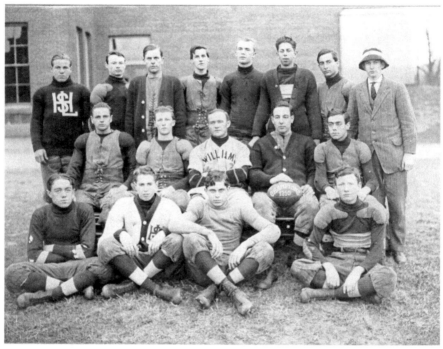

Undefeated 1910 Leominster High School Football team, captained by the legendary Lou Little. Little is seated, holding the football.

Lou Little during his coaching days at Columbia University.

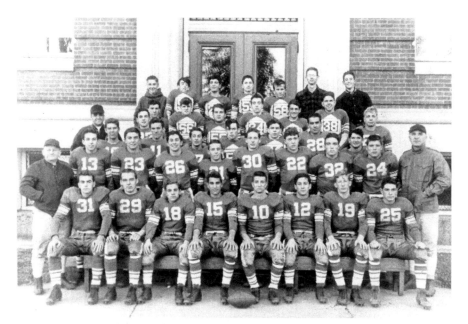

Leominster High School 1947 team photo. Future Fitchburg High School coach Marco Landon (seated wearing number 10) and future Leominster High School coach Leon "Huck" Hannigan (second row center, wearing number 21) would lead their respective teams to many Thanksgiving Day games, including a dramatic contest in 1969.

— *Chapter Seven* —

The Rivalry Sputters as the Twentieth Century Dawns

Enthusiasm for football and the competition between Leominster and Fitchburg High Schools on the gridiron dampened during the first few years of the new century. While the *Fitchburg Sentinel* was referring to the high schools as "old-time rivals" in 1898, the continuation of the competition was not accompanied by the sense of inevitability that the series carries today. Leominster and Fitchburg did not face each other in 1900 or 1902. In the long history of their rivalry, the familiar foes failed to meet on the football field in but three seasons: the two aforementioned years, as well as in 1923.

Legend has it that the 1923 game was the casualty of a fight that erupted during a basketball game between the schools in the spring of that year. In later years, witnesses recounted that Leominster star athlete James "Red" Barrett was constantly elbowing a Fitchburg player named Beach during a game in the basement drill hall of the old Leominster High School on West Street. Fitchburg's coach, Clarence Amiott, uncharacteristically authorized Beach to slug him on the chin if Barrett continued. Beach took Amiott's advice and knocked Barrett's two front teeth out. Barrett, who was a member of the 1923 graduating class of Leominster High School, went on to a football career at Harvard as a star tackle. Barrett's accomplishments at Harvard were rewarded in 1929, when he was unanimously elected the Harvard captain.

The situation worsened when Leominster High's Principal Smith inquired about Beach's participation in a basketball tournament at Tufts later in the season. Fitchburg's principal, Charles Woodbury, considered the whole matter an affront, noting that it was clear that Beach was entitled to the benefit of "the one slug per season rule" that was particular to high school basketball. After Principal Smith's inquiry, Fitchburg authorities voted to sever athletic relations with Leominster High without providing a formal reason.[55] Leominster had not managed a single victory over Fitchburg in the years between 1913 and 1924. Dejection must have described those years but, despite the dearth of success, somehow the Leominsters failed to give in. What remains to be explained is why the schools missed games in two of the first three years of the twentieth century.

As the new century dawned, peopled looked ahead. The December 1900 issue of the *Ladies Home Journal* contained a feature of what American's most-learned minds envisioned for the year 2000. The predictions ranged from super-sized (no, not fast-food meals) fruits and vegetables to instantaneous world communication and the eradication of insect pests. The experts thought that all cities would have a public gymnasium and a man or woman unable to walk ten miles would be considered a weakling. Whether the residents of Leominster and Fitchburg thought their high schools would still be sending teams to the gridiron is unknown. Automobiles were a novelty, and some eight thousand cars shared limited surfaced roads of the nation with innumerable horse-drawn carriages.

As autumn of 1900 approached, America turned its attention to national politics. The incumbent Republican President William McKinley was opposed by the Democratic nominee, William Jennings Bryan. Once again, the candidates who also faced each other in 1896 would debate monetary policy, and once again, McKinley would prevail. Locally, the fall season revealed a growing interest in football.

On September 27, the *Leominster Enterprise* posted an editorial question regarding the sport. The passing years and the question revealed a changing attitude toward football. The editor's query involved the

---

55   *Fitchburg Sentinel*, March 26, 1923.

town's lack of a club football team, a team comprised of young men of various ages already out of high school.

A Fair Question

> If Leominster is large enough to have two or three baseball teams, why is it not large enough to set up a football team? Many who played football and others interested in the sport are asking the question. There seems to be plenty of good material for a team that could equal any town team in the county and it is only a matter of getting things started to make it a success. Football is not dying out, as some think, but if anything is on the increase and Leominster should have a team in the field this fall.[56]

The editorial worked. Within a week, the Leominster Town Team announced a lineup and schedule. The roster included many names familiar to Leominster High School squads of the nineteenth century, including the 1894 team. The line would include Foster, Hadley, Metcalf, and Mahan. Mulqueeny, Richardson, and McCarthy would tote the pigskin. Unfortunately, the Leominster Town Team of 1900 disbanded before November and before ever playing any of its scheduled games. A town team could not exist without the ability to host games. The only available playing field was the driving park, and the high school team had primary control of the facility. The new team simply had no place to accommodate its home games.

Leominster High School's schedule was announced in September. The slate of games for 1900 included a Thanksgiving Day clash with Fitchburg. Leominster started its season with two new coaches, both of whom were medical doctors. Dr. T. H. Huchins, a graduate of Dartmouth, maintained medical practice in Leominster. His fellow coach, Dr. Richards, had come to Leominster to associate with Dr. Huchins just a month before the two physicians launched their coaching careers.

Early results for Leominster were promising. The team defeated the

---

56   *Leominster Enterprise*, September 27, 1900.

high schools of Maynard, Groton, and Concord without permitting any of those opponents to score a point. On Saturday, October 27, Leominster faced its first significant test when it faced a heavy Hudson team whose line averaged an astounding (for the times) 190 pounds. The lighter Leominster eleven were soundly defeated by a score of 46–0. Difficulties of a different nature loomed for the Fitchburg High team.

The October 29 edition of the *Fitchburg Sentinel* announced, "The (Fitchburg) football team will suspend its practice and games for the present until such time as some of the members elevate their low standing. All games are canceled for the next two weeks." With at least a temporary disbanding of the Fitchburg squad, Leominster went in search of a new Thanksgiving opponent to replace their neighboring rival. Leominster would arrange a Thanksgiving game with Worcester High School that year, which was confirmed by the Worcester manager when a rumor circulated that his team was backing out of its game with Leominster to pursue an opportunity to play the Yale University freshmen.

While the Leominster and Fitchburg upperclassmen never competed in 1900, the schools' freshmen teams did. The freshmen teams met each other three times that season—well, sort of. In the first two games, the teams split, and each squad prevailed in the contest played on their home turf. In their last contest, or "rubber match," the Leominster freshmen faced Fitchburg's freshmen and sophomores at their Circle Street grounds. Led by their star running back, Charles Kendall, Fitchburg came away victorious by a score of 31–5 on November 13, 1900.

Leominster faced additional inequities during the 1900 season. The composition of rosters and player eligibility continued to plague high school football into the twentieth century. When Leominster lost to Gardner High School by a score of 31–0, claims were made that the "Chair City" team had unenrolled players on its roster. A certain amount of vindication could be found in an article titled "Football Boys in Trouble" published in the *Leominster Enterprise* on November 8. The Gardner High School principal disciplined his school's team for permitting outside boys to play on the Gardner High team.[57] Eligibility concerns aside, both Leominster and Fitchburg High Schools

---

57   *Leominster Enterprise,* November 8, 1900.

turned their attention to Thanksgiving as trees went bare and cold November winds hinted at winter's approach. Fitchburg High School "having raised their grades satisfactorily" resumed football practice on November 20 in preparation for its Thanksgiving Day game with the Crescent Athletic Club of Clinton. As the team scampered off to practice, they may have snacked on a Pennsylvania chocolatier's brand-new confection, the Hershey bar. Leominster was in full anticipation of the arrival of the Worcester High team.

Thanksgiving morning brought fair weather. Prior to taking the field, the players of Worcester High and the host team would parade around Leominster, one team on "Parker's tally ho and the other in his brake." The Leominsters brought along a bass, a number of kettle drums, and a tuba, creating a clamor to stir the streets around the town center and driving park into a crowd of onlookers. The Leominster team had the pleasure of "banging their drums after the game in honor of their victory" by a score of 15–0. Fitchburg lost its holiday game 6–0. Early in the contest, Charles Kendall, the hero of the freshman contest with Leominster, broke free on a long scamper but slipped and fell before reaching the goal. The *Fitchburg Sentinel* lamented that the balance of the game displayed a rather "poor generalship" on the part of the hometown team. Fitchburg had previously declined an invitation to play Keene High School Thanksgiving afternoon and the opportunity to schedule a football "doubleheader." One game must have seemed rigorous enough, or perhaps the Fitchburg team was a bit disappointed that the morning's loss could not be redressed by an afternoon contest with the New Hampshire gridders. The 1900 season ended, and the Leominsters and Fitchburgs had failed to settle the annual accounting of the relative merit of their football teams.

The rivalry was reestablished in 1901. Once again, the office of president was in the news during the fall of that year. This time, however, the attention was not an election. On September 6, Leon Czolgosz, an American anarchist, shot President McKinley at the Pan-American Exposition in Buffalo, New York. McKinley died on September 14, becoming the third U.S. president to die at the hand of an assassin. Vice President Theodore Roosevelt, hero of the Spanish-American War, succeeded to the presidency. The next year, on September 2, 1902, President Roosevelt would address a crowd at Carter Park, the LHS football team's practice field, becoming the only sitting president to ever visit Leominster. Against the backdrop of national tragedy, the ebb and flow of life would continue. The autumn would bring the harvest scythe and the bell opening the new school term. High school fellows would eagerly await news of the college football season and turn their attention to forming their own teams. Fitchburg High began the 1901 season with the same questions that haunted the start of the prior football campaign. The FHS yearbook noted, "As the season opened, there were grave doubts as to whether there was any possibility of having a team, there was a great lack of suitable material with which to form a good one." The Fitchburg high schoolers of the early twentieth century simply had no interest in being embarrassed on the gridiron. At least some potential players were prepared to forego the sport altogether rather than field a team that was less than dominant. Before much more time passed, the talent was reassessed and Coach R.T. Sheehan was recruited, taking the reigns from James Hogan, who led the 1900 contingent. Coach Sheehan was a member of the FHS '97 eleven and a star tackle of Brown University's '00 squad—a team that faced and lost to powerful Harvard and Pennsylvania. Some of the players Coach Sheehan had to mold into an effective team included "Giant Barker," "Big Geoffrion," and "Slow but Sure Knight."

Perennial power Cushing Academy handed FHS a defeat in the season opener, where the vanquished, who lost 27–0, "were treated like gentlemen, but kindly shown (their) slight defects."[58] Fitchburg's second game on October 5 resulted in a 17–0 loss to Gardner. This time, the class yearbook remarked, as a number of sources were wont to do concerning Gardner's behavior of those years, that the loss was, "through no fault of ours, having been treated very discourteously by a series of foul decisions." Fitchburg got its revenge. In their second game with Gardner High School, the Fitchburg boys literally drove the Gardner team from the field after only ten minutes of the first half (teams were scheduled to play two twenty-minute halves), with Fitchburg having already tallied eleven points to Gardner's none. The Chair City eleven of Gardner, "fearful of a heavier defeat,"[59] simply walked off the field.

---

58   Fitchburg High School Yearbook, 1902, 19.
59   *Fitchburg Sentinel*, November 14, 1901.

Fitchburg's last of six games was played on November 9 and resulted in a win over Ayer High School. Sandwiched between the two Gardner matches and the first and last games of 1901 were two back-to-back games, games three and four, with Leominster. On October 9, Fitchburg "administered" the "plucky" Leominster team a 7–0 defeat. Ten days later, the Leominster boys hosted Fitchburg and returned the favor in a "game fairly and honestly won" by a score of 5–0. The season, which almost never happened, ended with Fitchburg earning an even 3–3 record in a campaign that lasted just a bit more than five weeks.

Fitchburg High School did not play a Thanksgiving game in 1901, and when the season ended, the team's quarterback, Hinrich, nicknamed "Little Duke" for reasons now unknown, and other underclassmen could look forward to a new year and a new football season in 1902. January 1, 1902 inaugurated one of college football's greatest events, the Rose Bowl, in Pasadena, California. Michigan defeated Stanford University in that first Rose Bowl by a convincing tally of 49–0. The thirty-second edition of that venerable college bowl game would help shape the reputation of a college hall of fame coach who would forever be endeared to Leominster citizens as one of their own. Coach Lou Little, who, as a player would lead Leominster to an undefeated 1910 season, also coached his alma mater in 1912. Little, along with John Heisman, who took the coaching reigns at Georgia Tech in 1904, and Jim Crowley, one of Notre Dame's famed Four Horsemen, comprised a panel appointed by the Downtown Athletic Club of New York City in 1935 to approve the design of a new college football trophy, which would ultimately take its name from Coach Heisman when he died the following year.

Little's appointment to the trophy panel came fresh after his coaching contribution to one of college football's greatest upsets. Lou Little coached Columbia, and the team's 1933 performance earned it an invitation to face Stanford University in the 1934 Rose Bowl. Almost immediately, the prospective game was declared a mismatch of epic proportions. Some oddsmakers predicted a sixty-plus point victory by Stanford. So great was the perceived disparity that Columbia's dean refused to permit his team's acceptance of the bowl invitation, fearing certain embarrassment. Coach Little refused to let the opportunity slip away and prevailed upon Columbia's dean to permit the game.

On January 18, 1934, Lou Little arrived by train at Worcester's Union Station. As he stepped off the platform, he gazed at a large crowd. It took him a few moments to realize that the assemblage was there for him. A cavalcade led the victorious coach who, ten days before, had led the underdog of underdogs to a 7–0 victory over powerful Stanford University. Leominster was already frenzied by the coach who sent greetings to his hometown during the post-game radio interview. It is said, by those who still remember, that Little's greeting created a collective cheer in the center of town that could be heard through windows closed against January's cold. By the time Little was conveyed from Worcester to Leominster for a banquet in his honor that evening, the entire town had emptied out into Monument Square. Fire alarms, church bells, factory whistles, and the cheers of thousands created a symphonic welcome for the man already well on his way to a legendary career.

The Fitchburg-Leominster game had already established itself as a tradition when the Rose Bowl got its start. Local football enthusiasts of the early twentieth century valued the tradition of the young series. The attachment to these games cannot be explained simply by past matches or geographic proximity. There was a simple emotional compulsion for the schools to compete which can be easily felt, but not so easily articulated, a condition that persists today. The failure of the rivals to meet in 1900 can be explained by a backlash that prioritized academics over football. More interesting questions arose during the 1902 football season.

From the beginning, 1902 was the tale of two teams. Leominster's season started with great promise and Fitchburg's did not. Fitchburg's Class Yearbook of 1903 looked back to the autumn of 1902 and observed that "the people of Fitchburg as a whole (did not) or (would) not take a just and natural interest in the doings of the high school and especially its athletics." It was left to the Class of '03 to revive the school's spirit, especially with a "great re-organization" of the football team near the season's end. Fitchburg's eleven were not as talented as the Leominster team in 1902, or at least that was the perception. A disparity in public support and coaching prowess did nothing to change that perception.

At the season's start, Coach Peter J. Dyer of Leominster pronounced that "the team of this year is the best in most respects that the school has ever had, they are putting up a better argument at football now than most teams have put up when the season is half over."[60] A month into the schedule, the opinion of Coach Dyer was as high. "Coach Dyer and the LHS eleven will teach the boys a new trick which he thinks is a winner. Dyer is a student of the game and has invented more than one play that has been successfully used."[61] The good feelings were reflected by game results. The Leominster team compiled a record of 7–1–1 in 1902, outscoring its opponents 191–33. Twenty-eight of the points given up came in their single loss to a powerful Waltham team.

Fitchburg's results, at least for the majority of the season, also met expectations. The Circle Street gridders lost five of their first six contests, prevailing only in a game against Lancaster High School on October 25 by a score of 34–0. Regardless of records or talents, scheduling a game between Leominster and Fitchburg was a question to be raised. Not surprisingly, the Leominsters struck first. "The Leominster boys would like to get after Fitchburg High School for a game and claim that they have used every means to bring about a meeting, but that for some reason the Fitchburg boys do not seem to care for a game. If they cannot arrange for a Saturday what's the matter with some Wednesday?"[62] The following Saturday, November 1, the Leominster team impressively dispatched with the Lowell High School contingent by a score of 28–0. In the wake of that game, one Leominster resident, not caught up in the football euphoria, took *Leominster Enterprise* to task.

> Editor of the Leominster Enterprise—I take the following from your edition on Saturday (November 1, 1902): "Considerable money will exchange hands on the result of the football game between the Lowell and Leominster High Schools. A large crowd should witness the sport.

---

60 *Fitchburg Sentinel,* October 3, 1902.
61 *Fitchburg Sentinel,* October 28, 1902.
62 *Fitchburg Sentinel,* October 28, 1902.

The interest we take in our high school leads us to hope that both for our reputation at home and abroad, it was not necessary or intentional to advertise the betting opportunities of our high school athletics as a leading feature of the game. Would it not be well, while we are demanding from our cashiers of our banks, and those whom we elect to public office of trust, freedom from the gambling spirit, that we do not encourage it in the young men whom we are educating?

Yours Respectfully, Frank J. Whitney
Leominster Enterprise, November 6, 1902

Gambling opportunities aside, at least the Leominster high schoolers continued to pursue their successful season as well as a game with their neighbors from Fitchburg. The contest would be confined to the newspapers only. For the second time in three years, Fitchburg and Leominster would not meet on the gridiron. At this writing, the ancient rivalry is at least 114, perhaps 115 years old. With the exception of the aforementioned 1923 season, these teams would never fail to meet again. In 1902, Fitchburg could only preserve its honor in newspaper articles that detailed scheduling difficulties. On Tuesday, November 11, Leominster responded to the notion that a game could not be arranged. "Notwithstanding the statement published by the Fitchburg correspondent to the *Worcester Telegram* regarding the great regret that a Fitchburg game could not be arranged between the high school of that city and this town, it remains a fact the Leominster did its best to get a game and if Fitchburg is very anxious to play Leominster a game can be arranged—in fact, nothing would please Leominster more."[63]

Leominster would not be pleased, and Fitchburg's anxiety would not find relief. Both schools would have to satisfy their competitive urges with a familiar foe, Gardner High. Both Leominster and Fitchburg faced Gardner High School twice in 1902. Leominster played Gardner to a scoreless tie on Gardner's home turf during their first meeting. The game ended with Gardner on the Leominster ten-yard line and the home crowd displeased with the officiating. In their second

---

63   *Fitchburg Sentinel*, November 11, 1902.

meeting, the larger Gardner boys were defeated by a smaller, quicker, well-disciplined Leominster team on Leominster's Green Street field by a score of 16–5. Gardner was so incensed that they sought a third Leominster game and in preparation called back a telephone linesman named Judino, who left his full-time job for a new round of course work at Gardner High and a night job as a telephone operator. The third game was never played.

Fitchburg played its first game of the 1902 season with Gardner on November 12, losing 18–6. Fitchburg played its second game with Gardner, and it's last game of the season, after the "Great Reorganization." The new regime included a new coach and the assembly of a scout team made up of volunteer Fitchburg High School boys who were not members of the football team. "The boys responded nobly and found themselves in the not-any-too-gentle hands of (the) new coach." According to the FHS 1903 class yearbook, "(T)he result was instantaneous! Much to our surprise, it was discovered that some of the new material was better than the old." The newly invigorated FHS football team earned a moral victory, playing a tough Gardner team to a scoreless tie on November 22.

The inhabitants of the Town of Leominster and the City of Fitchburg could be thankful for much as Thanksgiving 1902 approached. Two former football players from the LHS and FHS 1894 teams were already well into their careers. Mark O'Toole held a steady job as a mechanic at B.F. Blodgett Horn Company. Clifford Godbeer advanced his railroad career by becoming a timekeeper in the engineer's office of the Fitchburg Railroad. Leominster High School's gridders turned their attention to a Thanksgiving game with the Holy Cross Preps. The game must have included a good deal of hard-nosed play, given the number of fights that ensued. The captains of each team were ordered off the field as a result of extracurricular violence. The fights spread into the stands, and the police had to follow players into the crowd in order to quell the disturbances. Leominster won the contest on the field by a score of 6–0, and the victors celebrated their win in Monument Square with waving flags and clanging cowbells.

Any lingering doubt over the fate of football would not last long. If support and talent flagged in 1902, the shortcomings would be short-lived. Fitchburg's football program would take on the strength and character of so many other Fitchburg institutions during its golden age. The rival schools played thirty games between 1903 and 1924. Fitchburg defeated Leominster in nineteen of those games and tied an additional five contests. At one point during this era of dominance, Leominster would not earn a victory in fifteen games played over eleven straight years between 1913 and 1924.

These were formative years, not just for the rivalry, but for the game itself. The sport, not just the rivalry, would need its own rescue. Traditional competition among colleges and high school rivalries would provide a measure of staying power to a sport that sorely needed it in the early years of the twentieth century. Not long after the 1902 season faded, football itself would come under an attack that involved the highest authorities in the nation. Whatever the future of Fitchburg and Leominster's rivalry, the sport itself would engender a debate that threatened its very survival.

— *Chapter Eight* —

Football's Greatest Crisis

From the front page of the *Leominster Enterprise*, Monday, November 13, 1902:

Players on the Grid
Weeks Ago the Season Opened and Is Now Under Full Sway.

Weeks ago the season opened
For the players on the grid.
And by hundreds they enlisted,
Each for laurels making bid.
Some were types of manly beauty,
All were in the best of trim,
Every candidate for honors
Being sound in wind and limb.

But the changes have been many,
Since the starting of the fray;
Many faces now are missing
When the time is called for play.
Some in hospitals are lying,
Often giving vent to groans,
As they feel the painful twinges
In their slowly knitting bones.

Some are going 'round on crutches,
Every step denoting pain;
Here and there a convalescent
Only needs the aid of cane.
There are those who are nursing
Arms they're carrying in slings,
And they're shunning all crowds, fearing
Contact with their crippled wings.

But the veterans are lining
Up as boldly as before;
Every muscle they are straining
In their eagerness to score.
They've been toughened by the jostling
And the bumps they had to share,
But each one of them is showing
The effects of wear and tear.

Here and there an ear is missing,
Or a nose is turned awry,
Here and there are twisted fingers,
Here and there a bandaged eye.
Some around the field are limping,
There are many stiff and sore,
Yet in all the plays they're mixing,
For they're gritty to the core.

But before the season's over,
There'll be others borne away.
Bruised and shaken, torn and crippled,
From the scene of fearful fray.
Many heroes will be missing
When is raised the final shout,
For veterans in football
There'll be few to muster out.

Herbert Burgess played an entire game of football for Leominster High School on Wednesday, November 22, 1905. His team was defeated on its home turf by Worcester's Highland Military Academy by a score of 11–0. None of this was very remarkable except Burgess wasn't feeling very well by the time he arrived home that evening. No one remembered the football player taking any especially hard blow or going down with an injury. The newspaper reported, "When he was injured (he) must have pluckily kept the seriousness of it to himself." But injured he was. "He played the game through and afterwards went home, being in a bad way when he arrived home." Dr. A.H. Pierce was summoned and "discovered the real seriousness of the case."[64]

The exact outcome of Burgess's apparent concussion is lost to history. Nevertheless, he was lucky. During the era in which he played, when the professional game was practically nonexistent, deaths resulting from intercollegiate and high school football were all too common.

In 1905, a staggering number of football players died from injuries suffered on the gridiron. Some estimates of player deaths, which included collegiate, interscholastic, and club football players across the nation, ranged as high as one hundred. Whatever the debate there might be over the statistics, it is clear that at least nineteen of America's young men died playing intercollegiate football in 1905. The grim statistics were made worse when journalists brought to light the intentional nature of some of the violence. Early in 1905, Henry Beach Needham wrote a two-part article on the darker side of football for *McClure's Magazine*. In a Dartmouth-Princeton football game, the star player for Dartmouth was sidelined early in the game with a broken collarbone. The injured player was a black man, and the Princeton player who inflicted it was accused by a Harvard player and former prep-school teammate, himself black, of a racial motivation for the aggression. The Princeton player denied any racial motive and replied that he was coached to pick out the opponent's impact player and "put him out in the first five minutes." The article further damaged football's image with tales of additional scandal, including payoffs, cash-backed player recruitment, and disregard for eligibility rules.[65]

---

64 *Fitchburg Sentinel*, November 23, 1905.
65 Needham, *McClure's Magazine*, Volume 25, Issue 3, July 1905.

The football season in autumn of 1905 brought the attention of President Theodore Roosevelt, whose son was playing for the Harvard freshman football team. Just a few towns away from Leominster and Fitchburg, the president's friend Endicott Peabody served as the headmaster of the Groton School. Peabody introduced Roosevelt to the notion of a meeting of eastern college representatives and preparatory school headmasters for the purpose of football reform. On October 9, a group of football insiders from prominent programs met with the president, who expressed his concerns regarding the shortcomings of the game. Roosevelt succeeded in securing a pledge condemning brutality and unfair play; however, the words did little to change the course of the game or stem the carnage.

One death in particular began the push for real change. Harold Moore, a Union College football player, died after being kicked in the head during a game with New York University in the focal 1905 season. Moore's death prompted New York University's Chancellor Harry M. MacCracken to summon representatives from thirteen colleges to a reform conference in New York on December 5. One of the conference-attending schools, Columbia, had already abolished football less than two weeks before. What few modern football fans realize is that the conference, attended by some of the most important college football schools in the country, came within a single vote of abolishing the game, which at the time had no viable professional counterpart. Instead of abolishing the sport altogether, the conference planned for a larger convention later in the month that would include more than sixty schools.

After the larger conference convened, but before it finished its work, Harvard joined Columbia in abolishing its football program. Harvard's President Charles Elliot was no supporter of the game, and the school's overseers concurred in January of 1906. The *Sentinel* reported the dramatic news on Thursday, January 16, 1906:

> The overseers accepted unanimously the opinions of a special committee that the game as at present played is essentially bad in every respect; that the method of formation absolutely encourages trickery and foul play, and that the result is bad morals of the players

as well as for the body. The committee declared that if changes were to be made no man now a member of the so-called intercollegiate rules committee believing that these persons are so far committed to the present system that they could not agree to such changes as are absolutely necessary to produce a decent, clean, pleasurable contest, "instead of the present apology for a rough and tumble fight."

The Harvard overseers had at least part of the story right. A certain contingent of the conference attendees did not want radical changes that would transform football into a polite, emasculated game, including such far-reaching ideas as the forward pass. Yet a number of the representatives were ready to embrace real change. The division cleaved the conference into two separate committees that held a series of simultaneous New York meetings. Football's future hung precariously in the balance, and Americans had a variety of positions. Did our schoolboy football pioneers, Clifford Godbeer and Mark O'Toole, who ground out, literally, that "first" game a dozen years before, embrace the novel forward pass? While we will never really know, their nascent efforts, so important to what came after, make it deserving of at least the passing thought.

Harvard's support was courted by the conference. Without football at Harvard, it was much easier for other colleges to abandon the sport. Harvard's football coach, Bill Reid, attended the conference on behalf of the Harvard Crimson. Reid, the first salaried coach at Harvard, was hired by the college for the 1905 season. Reid was an alumnus who graduated with the class of 1901.

A love of football, then as now, can never be complete outside the context of a good rivalry. In the book *Big Time Football at Harvard 1905,* Reid is quoted as saying, "I don't see how a man can help feeling that hardly anything is more important than to beat Yale." Reid knew a little about competing with Yale. In 1898, a year marked by Leominster's controversial "loss" at Fitchburg, Reid led Harvard with two touchdowns in a 17–0 victory over Yale. The win was only the second time in eighteen seasons that the Crimson prevailed over Yale's

Eli. In his first coaching debut as an unpaid alum, Reid led Harvard to a perfect 17–0 season, culminating with a 27–0 defeat of Yale.[66]

Reid, who was among the group that met with President Roosevelt in October 1905, met twice more with President Roosevelt that year. On one occasion, he was called to the White House to answer to the president for Harvard's violation of the earlier pledge against violence. The president quizzed Reid about the expulsion of Harvard's center for slugging a Penn player during the Crimson's 12–6 loss. Reid asked Roosevelt, "What would you say if I told you that the Penn lineman was kicking our man in the groin?" The former Rough Rider, now president, responded, "What I would say would not be fit to print." Reid, who enjoyed a good dose of presidential access, would play a key role in the January 1906 conference.

Bill Reid left the old guard and joined the new committee. The move was a precursor to a merger of the two committees, which culminated with Reid replacing Walter Camp as the secretary of the new joint rules committee. The Joint Rules Committee was the forerunner of the National Collegiate Athletic Association (NCAA).

The replacement of Walter Camp, the "father of American football," signaled that real reform was in the offing. Camp himself was not opposed to all changes instituted by the new committee. In fact, he previously had suggested the change, ultimately adopted in 1906, which expanded first-down yardage from five yards to ten. The object was to open up the game with plays, such as end sweeps, designed to gain larger chunks of yardage and diminish the grueling, tight, hard-fought formations. Other members had bigger ideas to open up the game, most notably with the adoption of the forward pass.

Camp's dismay regarding the novel forward pass was tempered by the significant restrictions placed on the new play. A pass had to be made at least five yards from the line of scrimmage and cross the line of scrimmage no more than five yards to the right or left of the center.

---

66 Bill Reid would end his coaching career at Harvard at the conclusion of the 1906 season after losing to Yale in his final game 6–0. Despite his 30–3–1 record, Reid considered his coaching efforts a failure for having lost to Yale in 1905 and 1906. Common to all rivalries, good records are no compensation for the loss of the only game that mattered.

If a pass fell incomplete without touching any player, the offense was required to turn the ball over to the opponent at the point where the pass was attempted. A pass touched by either team but not caught was a free ball to be recovered as a fumble. Forward passes were limited to twenty yards, and a pass that crossed the goal line on the fly was treated as a touchback. These limitations stunted the popularity of the forward pass, especially with the older and more conservative colleges of the East, where Camp's influence was greatest. The more progressive schools of the Midwest and South were the first to experiment with the new offensive weapon. In addition to the forward pass and an increase in the yardage required for a first down, the Joint Rules Committee proposed seventeen additional changes, which Coach Bill Reid advised were necessary to continue football at Harvard (whose prestige was needed to save the game). The other rule changes included:

- Create a neutral zone the length of a football to separate lines and diminish the chance of violence;
- Restrict motion before the snap to one man;
- Establish a fair catch by the wave of a hand;
- Restrict the number of men behind the line to four, unless outside the ends, to eliminate mass-momentum plays;
- Increase the distance between the goal posts to twenty-five feet in order to encourage the kicking game;
- Allow no interference with a free kick;
- Allow no punt out for a try at goal. The try at goal or "extra point" (which was changed from two points to one in 1898) would be from a fixed spot centered before the goal posts, and the team scoring a touchdown would no longer be required to punt out the ball from the point where the ball crossed the goal line, scoring the touchdown for the purpose of centering the ball for the "try at goal;"
- Establish a second umpire to enforce player conduct;
- Ensure that the headlinesman monitor and penalize

offsides and illegal formations;

- Ensure that players be instantly disqualified for brutality, roughness, and insulting talk and no substitute be permitted for five minutes;
- Establish that a player disqualified a second time shall not play for one year;
- Establish that offense not hold, block, or otherwise obstruct opponents except with the body;
- Establish that the player with the ball can obstruct tacklers with the hand (straight arm);
- Establish that the penalty for the offensive holding shall be loss of the ball;
- Establish an on-side kick from any place on the field; the ball could be recovered by the offense provided it traveled twenty yards;
- Reduce the length of the game from two thirty-five minute halves to two thirty-minute halves; and
- Outlaw crawling with the ball, hurdling, and tripping.

What the committee did not change, despite prior suggestions to open up play, was the width of the field. Harvard's grand new stadium, opened in 1903, could not have accommodated a wider playing surface. All of the major eastern schools, except Columbia, followed Harvard's lead in endorsing the new proposals, and football narrowly averted its demise.

The newly modified game was met with a generally favorable acceptance, and for a time, injuries did diminish. True to Walter Camp's prediction that eastern colleges would not use the forward pass, the first college to put the forward pass to a real test in 1906 was a midwestern school, St. Louis University. Eddie Cochems, who gained great notoriety for his successful pioneering of the passing game, coached St. Louis. Following closely behind Cochems were coaching legends Alonzo Stagg of Chicago and Gene Scobie "Pop" Warner of the Carlisle Indian School. College programs were not the only football teams to experiment with the use of the forward pass.

The rule changes of 1906 were not long settled before their impact reached interscholastic football. The traditional Thanksgiving game between Leominster and Fitchburg saw the use of the forward pass for the first time in 1906. Both John Mulqueeny, who coached Leominster that season, and Coach Waters used the forward pass in the 1906 season. Each coach spent the early days of the 1906 season teaching their boys the new rules. The *Fitchburg Sentinel* reported Leominster's progress. "On account of the radical changes this season in football rules and the fact that the local season will open two weeks from today, the Coach (Mulqueeny) has not had time to devote to the rudiments of the game …"[67] On September 17, the *Sentinel* reported that during Fitchburg's early practices, directed by Coach John Waters, "a lot of attention will be paid to the forward pass which is difficult to perfect and entirely new." On Thanksgiving 1906, both Leominster and Fitchburg employed the pass, and while most of the passes were completed for little gain or not completed at all, Fitchburg did complete a pass for a touchdown, winning the contest at the Circle Street grounds 17–0. The following season would feature a Thanksgiving game between Leominster and Fitchburg that not only included novel rules but also the benchmark for competition.

Thanksgiving morning in north central Massachusetts dawned with threatening clouds and frozen, snow-covered ground in 1907. Leominster Coach Lawrence Duffy, previously the football coach of Boston English High School, watched approvingly as the early morning clouds melted away to reveal fair weather. The idea of a traditional Thanksgiving football game between Leominster and Fitchburg, which began just four years earlier, had already gained great favor. The *Fitchburg Sentinel* reported, "Both schools look forward to it as the one game of the year, and all others as but preparatory contests. The excitement was high when Fitchburg Coach, John Waters, his captain, George Wise and the remaining Fitchburg warriors arrived at Leominster's old athletic grounds."[68] The field was cleared by the highway scraper, and the spectators totaled 2,500, probably the largest crowd to ever watch a football contest in Leominster to that time. "They came in all sorts of vehicles and conveyances. There were hundreds of automobiles

---

67   *Fitchburg Sentinel*, September 11, 1906.
68   *Fitchburg Sentinel*, November 29, 1907.

and teams of all descriptions."[69] The faithful predicted a close game and a low score. Leominster's season had included only one loss, and Fitchburg won six contests by shutout against just two losses to strong Waltham and Lowell High School teams.

As the day warmed, the field softened, making footing less than ideal. Leominster's line play was stronger and the offense had some success; however, Fitchburg's defense stiffened when its back was against the wall. The *Fitchburg Sentinel* added its own view of Leominster's offense:

> At the conclusion of the first half the only criticism of Leominster team that might be made was that they had been taught too many new plays in the last few days. They had a numerous assortment of trick plays they had never tried in a game before. They were clever and many of them worked to perfection ...[70]

Six minutes into the game, Fitchburg's punt receiver fumbled a punt from Leominster's Wass on the Fitchburg thirty-five-yard line. The *Fitchburg Sentinel* captured the resulting drive: "a forward pass and an onside kick (both features of the 1906 rule changes) worked it to the thirteen yard line at the extreme right of the field. An end play carried it in front of the goal and on the next play Wass booted it between the posts."[71] The field goal scored four points, pursuant to the scoring values then in effect, and Leominster netted the only points of the first half.

Earlier in the 1907 season, Leominster also witnessed a liberal use of the forward pass in its contest with Hudson High School on Saturday, October 5. Hudson completed several passes for good gains; however, Leominster's running attack was too strong and the home team defeated Hudson 20–6. By November 11, in a match with Marlborough High School, Leominster was making good use of the forward pass, onside kicks, and the punting game. Leominster would continue its wide-open style of play in the second half of the

---

69   *Fitchburg Sentinel,* November 29, 1907.
70   *Fitchburg Sentinel,* November 29, 1907.
71   *Fitchburg Sentinel,* November 29, 1907.

1907 Thanksgiving game. Leominster possessed the ball most of the half, and when Fitchburg finally got its hands on the ball, the team failed to use the punting game to gain any field-position advantage. Despite Leominster's decided advantage in both field position and ball possession, Fitchburg's defense was able to keep the Leominster eleven from scoring. The final two minutes of play remained, and fans of both teams grew anxious as the seconds ticked away.

Leominster's quarterback, Bullard, waited as Fitchburg's Warner dropped back to punt. Warner's punt barely cleared the line and went bounding away toward the Leominster goal. Bullard watched the ball bounce and made a critical decision. Instead of falling on the ball, Bullard attempted to pick it up off the ground, fumbling it in the process. Once again, Bullard reached for the ball, but he had run out of time—a Fitchburg player arrived and cradled the ball on the Leominster thirty-five-yard line. Invigorated by their good fortune, Fitchburg advanced the ball to the Leominster twenty-yard line in two plays. Two successive running plays failed as Leominster's defense repelled the advances. On Fitchburg's third down, its captain, George Wise, drop-kicked a field goal from the twenty-five-yard line, tying the score 4–4. The *Fitchburg Sentinel* captured the visiting fans' jubilation: "Fitchburg supporters simply went crazy with joy. It was several minutes before the police were able to clear the field. After a kick-off, time was called with the ball in Leominster's possession at the center of the field."[72]

The Thanksgiving game of 1907, noteworthy for a display of football's new tactics brought about by the crisis of 1906, also in many ways cemented the Leominster-Fitchburg rivalry for all time. The *Fitchburg Sentinel* headlines captured the elevated mood:

Spectacular Contest
WITH HONORS EVEN
Capt. Wise of Fitchburg High by Brilliant Field
Goal Snatched Victory From Leominster
- - - Annual School Contest Approach-
es in Enthusiasm and Spirit
a College Game.

---

72 *Fitchburg Sentinel*, November 29, 1907.

Rescued and revived, college and interscholastic football provided a distraction from the drudgery of work and grim national events. For a few hours on Thanksgiving morning, none of the supporters of either team gave a thought to the bank failures of that fall, soaring food prices, or America's show of naval power under sail of the "Great White Fleet." Football, or more accurately, football rivalry, would forever alter the relationship between schools and colleges throughout the country. The link between Fitchburg and Leominster was inalterably changed by 1907. The rivalry born out of football created a competition that extended beyond the gridiron, and each community looked with pride to the institutions and public amenities that the wisdom of its leaders and the spirit of its citizens created. In time, and as each community grew, the municipal leaders turned their attention to providing proper facilities for athletics. Spurred by a pride that was no less connected to its high school football team than any other asset either boasted, each community looked progressively ahead.

—— Chapter Nine ——

A Year of Triumphs and Tragedy, 1918

"Crocker Field"
Oh! Here's to Alvah Crocker,
Generous and true!
Here's to the field
That he has given to you!
Long may his name be honored
Here and afar!
So—Three cheers for Crocker!
With a Rah! Rah! Rah!

(Sung to chorus of "Our Director March"),
Crocker Field Dedication, Friday, June 21, 1918

Workmen gazed over the large, flat expanse ringed by a substantial ornamental iron fence set in a running concrete base. The field house was nearly complete, and two permanent grandstands awaited spectators who someday would come to witness athletic events on the newly sown field. Laborers planted small American elms along the impressive fence, softening the encompassing barrier. In a matter of weeks, Fitchburg would unveil an athletic facility surpassed by few, if any, high school sports venues. The old Circle Street grounds, host to decades of athletic contests, had been transformed in a dramatic way.

The cool and rainy nights of late April nurtured the field's new cultivations. However the city was uneasy, the volume of news during the spring of 1918 extended far beyond local events. Each day was greeted with caution. On Tuesday evening, April 23, Will Ayer left his insurance firm, Faxon, Ayer & Smith, and returned to his residence at 4 Fairbanks Street. Later that evening, Mr. Ayer received an ominous telegram from the United States War Department. Will Ayer maintained a closely knit household. His nephew and two young nieces made their home with him. His nephew was currently with the U.S. Army in France, and the telegram from the War Department was not welcome news. His nephew, Lieutenant Lawrence S. Ayer, became the first Fitchburg boy killed in action during the World War. Lieutenant Ayer lost his life during the battle of Seicheprey in France on Saturday, April 20. Assigned to Battalion C, 103d Field Artillery, the lieutenant and American forces helped repulse 1,200 German storm troops, who were part of an effort to breach British and French lines in Flanders and take Paris before Americans could give substantial assistance to the allied cause. Before the armistice was signed on November 11, 1918, 116,000 American soldiers would die in the war.

The *Fitchburg Sentinel* announced that "news of his (Lieutenant Ayer's) death cast a gloom over the City."[73] City flags were lowered to half-mast to honor the fallen soldier. Lieutenant Ayer was born in December 1894 at Putman, Vermont. He came to Fitchburg in 1909 where he entered the Fitchburg High School and graduated in 1912 as the class president and valedictorian. During his high school years, he was a prominent athlete who "played baseball and basketball and was unusually proficient in both sports."[74] After high school, he entered Dartmouth and graduated from that college in 1916. When America's involvement in the war became likely, Lieutenant Ayer left his job at the Worcester firm of Grafton-Knight Company and enrolled at the Plattsburg School, where he was commissioned an officer in May of 1917. He was deployed to France in the fall of 1917 and arrived there on September 24.

The loss was keenly felt throughout the city. He was the first to fall. His death was made even more tragic by the respect and popularity he earned from his peers and those who knew him. During vacations from college, he served as a playground instructor and enjoyed mentoring

---

73   *Fitchburg Sentinel*, April 24, 1918.
74   *Fitchburg Sentinel*, April 24, 1918.

the youth of Fitchburg. There is little doubt that Lieutenant Ayer spent formative days on the baseball diamond at the Circle Street grounds. A few moments of recreation away from hostilities in France would have brought back a flood of memories from the primitive Fitchburg field that hosted the baseball exploits of his high school days. Less than two months after his death, Fitchburg dedicated its new field, a majestic achievement built upon that same ancient playing field. Those moments of celebration must have been tempered for Fitchburg residents, who remembered Fitchburg's first fallen soldier of the war still being waged on that June day.

The Fitchburg Military Band led a parade of faculty, alumni, city officials, and all the city's school children from Fitchburg High School across Main Street to the dedication of Crocker Field on Friday, June 21, 1918. The crowd, festooned with class banners and American flags, began its march with great anticipation at two o'clock sharp. The event was planned to coincide with the annual junior-senior city relay race, which inaugurated the new track that afternoon.

Before the race, the ceremonial portion of the afternoon commenced when the parading crowd arrived and assembled in place on the field and in the new grandstands. Mr. Crocker presented the keys to the field to Mayor Frank H. Foss, and the mayor accepted the field with an address that according to the newspaper was "brief and without (a) profusion (of) words for oratorical adornment."[75] Alvah Crocker was a public-spirited man, but he did not seek attention for his deeds. Mayor Foss and the *Fitchburg Sentinel's* editor understood Mr. Crocker's reluctance for accolades. The *Fitchburg Sentinel* coverage noted the brevity of the mayor's remarks. "Reticence in this respect was more befitting and the donor of the magnificent gift to the city was spared the embarrassment of hearing in his presence the sounding of fulsome praises."[76] The city's benefactor had the gratitude of the assembled saluting him in song and precisely executed wand drills.

Near the conclusion of the program, the crowd of four thousand, an enormous gathering for the time, rose in unison and saluted the American flag with an emotion heightened by the war and a pride strengthened by common purpose. No one had ever witnessed

75 *Fitchburg Sentinel,* June 22, 1918.
76 *Fitchburg Sentinel,* June 22, 1918.

allegiance to the national standard recited by such a crowd, and no one present had experienced an athletic facility that remotely approached the splendor of Crocker Field.

The relay race followed the flag salute. The importance of this annual event is understood in part by the fact that a president, captain, manager, and coach led each team. The football coach, J.A. Chalmers, led the juniors, and George V. Upton Jr. led the senior team. Each team was comprised of thirty runners. The teams lined up before the unprecedented crowd on the brand-new track. History, pride, and luncheon for the winners were at stake. The coaches closely observed the physical condition of their charges, and all was readied for the event.

The gun sounded and Crocker Field's first great athletic contest was underway. The runners, spurred by an intense rivalry that was "a bit too spirited the evening before," gave their all and all were examined after the race, with only a few of the boys being "a little wobbly."

The seniors restored themselves over their prize luncheon, served by the school faculty in the new field house. A prior agreement gave the victors the privilege of flying their class flag over the high school after the race that Friday and the following Monday and Wednesday. The juniors, as a consolation, flew their banner during the intervening Tuesday.

The band serenaded the dining senior racers and the huge departing crowd. The throng emptied out onto Main Street in a jovial mood, contemplating the magnitude of what Fitchburg now possessed. Even then, those first spectators paused to reflect on the long future of sporting contests, drama, victory, and defeat that lay ahead. Alvah Crocker had already dreamed the future.

His ideas were launched with an announcement on Tuesday, January 2, 1917. The *Fitchburg Sentinel* carried a banner headline:

ALVAH CROCKER MAKES PRINCELY GIFT TO THE CITY
Proposes to Develop Circle Street Grounds Into Magnanimously Equipped Athletic Field and Turn it Over to the Public Schools, With Fund of $38,000.00 to Maintain It.

Crocker's letter to the city was reprinted beneath the headline:

ALVAH CROCKER'S LETTER TO THE MAYOR
AND COUNCIL.

Fitchburg, Mass., Jan. 1, 1917.

To the Mayor and City Council of the City of Fitchburg,
Massachusetts

Gentlemen:
In my opinion the public schools of the city require an
adequate field in which the different out-of-doors sports
and contests, which count so much in the physical and
moral development of our boys, can be held.

The importance of a thorough training in baseball,
football and other athletic sports is well recognized,
and I feel that what can be done to make such training
popular as well as more perfect, will be of great benefit
to our public spirit and civic unity.

I have recently acquired for this purpose, the title
of the Circle Street property, so-called, and now desire
to give it to the city of Fitchburg for the use of the
public schools.

If this gift is accepted by you on behalf of the city,
I shall proceed forthwith to have laid out a baseball
diamond, football field and running track. I propose
to build a locker building equipped with shower baths
and other usual conveniences. There will also be seating
arrangements for a limited number of spectators.
Plans for the arrangements of the grounds and for the
construction of the building have been prepared by
the landscape architects, Messrs. Olmsted Brothers of
Brookline, Mass., and these plans have already been
approved by competent experts. I shall hope with this
letter to submit to you a plan designed to give idea of
the field as it will look when completed.

It is my wish and request that this field shall be under the control and management of the school committee, or of such sub-committee as it may from time to time appoint.

I shall also deposit with the city treasurer in trust with authority to invest and reinvest, $38,000 in City of Fitchburg four per cent bonds, the income to be expended under the direction of the school committee towards the perpetual care of the property.

Respectfully yours,
ALVAH CROCKER.

Mr. Crocker's vision included facilities that, in the opinion of many, were comparable to the Worcester Academy, at the time considered to have the model athletic plant for preparatory schools in the country and, but for the size of grandstands, Harvard's Soldiers Field. The landscape architects, the Olmsted Brothers, had a resume that included landscape designs at the Harvard Business School, the University of Chicago, the University of Notre Dame, and Vassar College. Their landscape projects included scenic roadways in the Arcadia National Park, Yosemite Valley, and the Great Smoky Mountains.

The project was intended to create an asset, for the City of Fitchburg excelled in no other place. Crocker Field was a manifestation of pride and an investment in youth by a man who had accumulated abundant financial reward during Fitchburg's golden age. The *Fitchburg Sentinel* editor concurred with the donor and spoke for grateful residents. "This splendid endowment, in the spirit in which it is bestowed, and in the purposes for which it is intended, will be of immeasurable value in its influence for the good of the community."[77]

Success in business creates a moral re-examination. Andrew Carnegie, the rags-to-riches industrialist who rose to build U.S. Steel from a bobbin boy's meager wage, famously quipped, "No man can be rich until he enriches others." Put another way, the Bible asks "What good is it to gain the world and lose your soul?" Within days of the

---

77   *Fitchburg Sentinel*, June 22, 1918.

June 1918 dedication of Crocker Field, Alvah Crocker would have his faith tested.

The devastating news arrived with tactless insensitivity. Just days after the Crocker Field dedication ceremony, the Associated Press sent a brief cablegram. "Brest, France, Wednesday, June 26, Captain Alvah Crocker of Massachusetts died suddenly Tuesday." The *Fitchburg Sentinel* received the dispatch on Monday, July 1, 1918. When last heard from, Alvah Crocker 2nd was an army lieutenant serving with the U.S. Engineer Corps stationed at Brest, France. His parents had received no word of their son's fate, despite the fact that he had died nearly a week before the Associated Press announcement. A swirl of questions and disbelief punctuated each passing hour after the newspaper ran the front-page story on Monday morning. Mr. and Mrs. Alvah Crocker received a War Department telegram that evening confirming their son's death with the same cold shortness of the initial dispatch. "Deeply regret to inform you that it is officially reported that Lieutenant Alvah Crocker, Jr. Engineers died June 25."

In the span of nine days, the Crockers had experienced a grateful appreciation for their gift to the youth of Fitchburg for generations to come and the deep sorrow accompanying the loss of a child. Their son would never come home, never gaze upon the hills of Fitchburg, and never feel his parents' embrace again.

Alvah Crocker Jr., born in Fitchburg, attended the Groton School, where he starred on the baseball and football teams. After his graduation in 1900, Crocker went on to Harvard College, where he was a substitute on the football team during the 1904 season, just one year before the watershed year that prompted significant rules reform. After graduating with the class of 1905, he joined his father's paper-making firm, Crocker-Burbank Company. In 1909, Crocker left the family business to pursue an interest in art and architecture. When the war broke out, he was enrolled at the L'École Supérieure des Beaux Arts in Paris and near the completion of requirements for his diploma. The architecture student put his talents to work in the U.S. Army Engineer Corps., where he received a commission as a lieutenant.

The Crocker family was deeply involved in the war effort. On the home front, Alvah Crocker Sr. was the president of the Fitchburg Chapter of the Red Cross. The Crockers had four surviving children, two sons and two daughters. Douglas was a captain assigned as an instructor at Fort Sill, Oklahoma, and their other surviving son, John, was enrolled at Harvard. Daughter Helen was a Red Cross nurse and the wife of Dr. Willard Soper, both of whom were working for the war effort in France. The Crockers' other daughter, Charlotte Kelley, wife of Shaun Kelley, who was employed by a large banking firm in Paris, was home to comfort her parents in their grief.

Lieutenant Crocker left a wife and three children in France. The circumstances of his death were not immediately clear. Early reports surmised that the young man succumbed to disease, a fate not uncommon to World War I soldiers. Specifics of Crocker's death arrived by cablegram on Wednesday, July 3. Lieutenant Crocker had taken his own life. Official reports suggested the young soldier broke under the strain of an intense workload. The lieutenant's remains lie buried in France, laid to eternal rest with full military honors. The *Fitchburg Sentinel* reported that Crocker was "intensely sensitive in spirit, (and) suffered to the limit of human capacity and almost beyond it. Highly conscientious, he flung himself into his military and engineering tasks with a devotion that completely wore him out, and under the strain of sympathy and overwork, he broke as have many of the most conscientious and efficient officers in all the armies at war."[78] Fitchburg lamented the human loss associated with the war. The world war committee compiled the names of those Fitchburg residents who lost their lives while on active duty with the armed forces during the war. Sixty-three names joined those of Lieutenant Ayer and Lieutenant Crocker on the bronze memorial tablet. Like many wars, death came as often from disease and illness as from mortal wounds.

Thomas E. Moses, Machine Gun Class, Forty-Second Infantry, took ill during the waning days of September 1918. Moses was stationed at Camp Devens, only a dozen miles from his 37 Carey Street home. The Fitchburg boy never came home. Thomas Moses died at Camp Devens on October 2 from influenza. His death coincided with an influenza epidemic, which outstripped medical resources and sent scores to an early death. Panic gripped the local population as the pandemic emanating from Devens spread throughout Massachusetts and across the nation. American soldiers brought influenza back from

---

78   *Fitchburg Sentinel*, July 5, 1918.

the European War. The name Spanish influenza belied the origin of the sickness. Spain was not involved in the war. The name helped to avert panic from the essential origin of the influenza, the European War countries. Returning from the war, many American soldiers were processed for discharge through Camp Devens, and thus the military installation became ground zero for the pandemic.

A half million Americans died from the influenza before the outbreak ended in 1919. Locally, life changed. A few dozen hospital beds in Fitchburg and Leominster expanded to hundreds, as private homes and schools were hastily converted to accommodate the sick and dying. Schools, churches, theaters and other places of public assembly were closed to abate the spread of the contagion. Scores of Leominster and Fitchburg inhabitants died from the epidemic. Local bans and fear did not begin to subside until late October.

Football too was affected. Leominster's fielding of a football team was in doubt as the 1918 season dawned. The *Fitchburg Sentinel* reported that as of Wednesday, September 18, thirty candidates were out for the team, which lacked a coach and was yet to face the brunt of the influenza epidemic. Early season uncertainties forced Fitchburg High School to seek another Thanksgiving opponent for its first holiday tilt on Crocker Field. Powerful Peabody High School was scheduled in Leominster's place. Eventually, veteran Leominster Coach John P. Mulqueeney, who starred on the field at Holy Cross and Dartmouth, was recruited, and the team made strides and improvements.

Fitchburg began the season with all the promise of having one of the best athletic fields in the country could inspire. The team lost a month of practice to the influenza epidemic but managed to play a schedule of strong teams that included Malden, Manchester, New Hampshire, Lawrence, Peabody, and St. John's Prep. With the blessing of local health officials, the inaugural football game at Crocker Field pitted the home team against Malden High School on September 28. The home team led the scoring 7–6 late into the contest. With just a few minutes left, Malden had possession of the ball and was driving toward the Fitchburg goal. The visitors attempted a forward pass that was intercepted by Fitchburg's right halfback, Carpinella, who returned the ball fifty-five yards for a touchdown. The final tally, Fitchburg 13, Malden 6, was displayed on the brand new scoreboard, which carried a football outcome for the first time. The health officials may have been overly optimistic. Fitchburg didn't play another football game until October 27, canceling three games scheduled with Gardner, Everett, and Worcester High Schools.

Leominster's season got off to a slow start. LHS also had a new field. For the first time, Leominster would play its football games on the school campus field to the rear of the high school at the corner of Hall Street and Merriam Avenue. The city expended some $3,500 to fill a large depression behind the high school and grade the tight confines into a football field. The distinction between Leominster's facility and Crocker Field could not have been greater. Until Doyle Field was opened in 1931, Fitchburg refused to play on the Leominster field. It would be hard to blame them. The grandstands and facilities were small and initially lacked an enclosure that permitted enforcing an admittance fee.

Despite the sparse facility, Leominster's season was a success. Leominster played a short schedule of five games but lost only once. A game with Fitchburg was scheduled to take place at Crocker Field on November 2. Milford High School cancelled its game with Fitchburg, slated for November 9, since Milford had closed its schools in early November as a result of the influenza epidemic. Fitchburg suggested postponing the Leominster game to the Milford game date "to allow both teams to get in better condition and put up the best possible exhibition for their supporters."[79] Both teams were recovering from a lack of practice due to the influenza outbreak. The annual meeting of rivals did not take place until the Saturday before Thanksgiving. The teams would meet at Crocker Field for the first time on November 23, 1918.

Fitchburg was a heavy favorite, in part literally, since they outweighed their Leominster counterparts. Early football followers were obsessed with comparing teams' weights. More importantly, Fitchburg was a faster squad. Leominster's loss by a score of 20–0 was not unexpected, and the team earned a measure of respect despite the lopsided score. Fitchburg adopted a new custom when the Fitchburg High School band and students marched to Depot Square, where they boarded cars to Leominster's downtown. Once arrived, the jubilant representatives of Red and Gray paraded through Leominster's center, fortunately without incident. Leominster had not scored a single point against Fitchburg since 1912, when the Blue and White prevailed by a score

---

79   *Fitchburg Sentinel,* October 17, 1918.

of 19–0. In the ten games played between 1913 and 1918, there was a scoreless tie and only two games where Fitchburg's margin of victory was smaller than 1918's. In addition to a 1913 scoreless tie, Fitchburg beat Leominster in a second 1913 game, 13–0, and by the same score in one of the 1915 contests.

Leominster finished the 1918 season with a Thanksgiving game on its own new field. The Leominster warriors defeated the Worcester Trade School 20–0, despite the fact the visitors were permitted to play its prior-year graduates and players from other Worcester schools. Leominster completed a shortened schedule with a successful 4–1 record. Fitchburg faced off against powerful Peabody High School.

The Peabody team left for Fitchburg on a large autobus at 6:30 PM on Wednesday, November 27, arriving for an overnight stay at the Hotel Raymond just before 11:00 PM. The powerful Peabody eleven entered the grand football venue before an excited crowd of two thousand spectators. Peabody represented the class of the state and was planning to meet Marblehead High School for the state championship. Fitchburg struck first, scoring a touchdown in the second period after a sustained drive that featured a constant battering of the vaunted Peabody line by inspired Fitchburg players. Peabody was able to even the score with a last-period touchdown. The hometown supporters claimed satisfaction with the tie score, calling it "practically a victory."[80]

Fitchburg finished the eventful season with a 5–1–1 record, its only loss coming at the hands of Manchester High School. The Manchester coach joined Fitchburg's Coach Chalmers on the Fitchburg sideline Thanksgiving morning. He gratuitously admitted that the Red and Gray had improved enough to defeat his Manchester squad by that late point in the season. Fitchburg lost to Manchester by a score of 21–0 on November 2, shortly after Fitchburg had resumed its season.

It was a time to take stock. The year was one of triumph and tragedy. In a year marked by great loss, the inhabitants of Fitchburg, aided by the generosity of one man, had invested in youth and the future. Perhaps in an important way, Alvah Crocker's gift helped make some sense of it all. Crocker's vision captured a spirit that would permit a community to persevere and heal. The donation and dedication of Crocker Field could not have been more timely.

---

80   *Fitchburg Sentinel*, November 29, 1918.

Chapter Ten

Doyle Field :
Leominster's Time of Achievement and Loss

We may express our hope that the Doyle Field will become in the eyes of Leominster citizens as beautiful as Crocker Field is to Fitchburgers, and that it come to mean as much in the community life of Leominster as Crocker Field means in the community life of Fitchburg.

But we hope that they will never ask us to admit that the Leominster Field is the more beautiful or that the Leominster players are better than the Fitchburg players. *The rivalry must continue keener than ever, for it is a part of the spice of existence in the Twin Cities.* (emphasis added)

However Fitchburg is willing to grant at the outset as even contest in one important respect: that is, in the production of public spirited men like Mr. Doyle and Mr. Crocker whose generosity will benefit generations of men and women to come. Editor, *Fitchburg Sentinel*, Thursday, August 22, 1929

Mayor Doyle sat at his city hall desk reflecting on his years in office. The workload had taken its toll; he was tired. Four years as Leominster's chief executive, business duties, and dedication to civic projects combined with strenuous effect. The popular mayor was content with his decision. Bernard Doyle prepared a short press release. It was a direct and unequivocal message; he would not be a candidate for reelection to a third term, and his decision was final.

The *Fitchburg Sentinel's* front page carried Mayor Doyle's announcement on Friday, November 1, 1929. Above the photo of the bespectacled Honorable Bernard W. Doyle was the bold caption, "Will Not Run." That same edition of the newspaper carried another page-one story of strain and exhaustion. Thousands of clerks faced the daunting task of recording an unprecedented number of financial transactions. Wall Street brokerage houses worked feverishly to keep up, and the markets were closed for nearly two days of that week in an effort to recover. The market had *crashed* on Tuesday, October 29, Bernard Doyle's fifty-sixth birthday. Not even the most panicked Americans knew what lay ahead.

Leominster's municipal finances were in order. Mayor Doyle's message noted the city's "reasonable surplus" as well as a tax burden and indebtedness, within reasonable limits. The mayor thanked Leominster citizens for their confidence and its city council and public employees for their "splendid cooperation" and "keen interest in their work." One of those city councilors took up the mantle and announced his candidacy for mayor contemporaneously with Mayor Doyle's disclaimer of a third term. Council President Frederic T. Platt, a seven-year veteran of that body, voiced his preference for another Doyle term but accepted the request of his many supporters to run, given the incumbent's determination not to. Apparently, Mr. Platt's supporters were numerous enough to achieve his election as Leominster's mayor a little more than a month later on December 3, 1929.

The departing mayor would have more time to devote to an ambitious project that got underway during his last full year in office, 1929. Early that year, Doyle approached Raymond L. Middlemas, treasurer of the Leominster Savings Bank, with the idea of building a new athletic field for the high school and the city. Middlemas and Doyle were friends who also had a business relationship. While Middlemas was employed as an officer of the bank, Doyle sat on its board of trustees. In Middlemas, Doyle had a trusted confidant with honed business skills.

When the two men discussed the notion of a new athletic facility for Leominster, Doyle had already compiled a resume of breathtaking business, political, and civic achievements. His interest in sports was manifested by membership in at least ten sporting clubs, ranging from the Izaak Walton League-Links Club of New York City to the Corinthian Yacht Club of Marblehead and the Monoosnock Country Club of Leominster. His success was stunning but tempered by a desire to improve the lives of others and his community. Often, his largesse was quiet and unassuming; however, some of his generosity was of a scale that necessarily involved public collaboration. In 1919, Doyle donated twenty acres of land to construct a new hospital for Leominster, replacing the outmoded Blossom Street building that served as Leominster's hospital. That outmoded structure, which still stands today, accommodated less than 20 percent of the sick during the prior year's influenza outbreak, with its dozen or so beds.

Having grown up the son of a factory laborer, Doyle understood the needs of his community. His story is as much a Horatio Alger "rags-to-riches" account as any other. Born in 1873, he spent most of his school years on Mount Pleasant Avenue and nearby Wilson Street, both ways crossing a small hill to the southeast of Leominster's Town Center. His parents lost the home they owned, and the family lived in several apartments. Doyle graduated from Leominster High School with the class of 1891. That fall, while he traveled to the Eastman Commercial College of Poughkeepsie, New York, Leominster boys were already engaged in football games at Robbins' Driving Park. Always a lover of sport, the young student could not have imagined the role he would someday play in transforming that "old driving park" any more than he could imagine changes in football itself over the next four decades.

After a year's course of study in Poughkeepsie, in 1892, he returned to Leominster and a job at the Horn and Supply Company as a bookkeeper. As he was settling into his early career, Leominster's comb industry was already two centuries old. The town was dotted with numerous comb making concerns, large and small. These factories and others throughout the world created an ever-increasing demand for animal horn. Doyle's involvement in the horn industry quickly blossomed into the attainment of beneficial experience and valuable business acumen.

Alexander Patton, a colorful Scottish immigrant, bought the Horn and Supply Company in 1897. The association between Patton and Doyle was a significant turning point in the latter's career. Patton dispatched Doyle, who by the time of his departure was the company's secretary and general manager, to Europe as his agent to buy South American horn in the London market. The trip was a turning point. The young business executive was hard working, intelligent, and forward thinking. Only one ingredient was missing: in a single word, like the advice contained in a renowned quote from 1967's popular movie *The Graduate,* plastics!

Bernard Doyle would be introduced to a pioneering plastic compound, pyroxylin, on a visit to the Robert Ocshe Company in Paris. Within a few years, the Viscoloid Company was formed by partners Alexander Patton, Bernard Doyle, Ludwig Stross of New York, and Paul Rie of Paris to manufacture and improve plastic resin. Doyle's role and interest in the company grew, and by 1923, he was its chief executive. As Viscoloid's chief executive, he oversaw 1,800 employees on a sixty-acre manufacturing site containing forty-two buildings. In the same year, he was elected Leominster's mayor. In 1925, the Viscoloid Company was merged with DuPont Company of Wilmington, Delaware. The new entity would be known as DuPont Viscoloid Company, a subsidiary of E.I. DuPont deNemours and Company. Doyle would continue to serve the newly organized company as a vice president. His meteoric rise and stunning business success led Bernard Doyle, not unlike Alvah Crocker, to a consideration of other pursuits.

A proper athletic facility for the youth of Leominster was a natural outgrowth of his civic-mindedness, involvement in municipal politics, and love of sport. Raymond Middlemas and Bernard Doyle considered various sites for the athletic facility. The plan was ambitious. The plant, as sporting facilities were called in those days, would include multiple football and baseball fields, a soccer field, track, skating and hockey rink, tennis courts, playground, and parking. The men settled on a large twenty-acre parcel that would include the old Robbins driving park and adjoining land with streets already laid out for housing but still mostly undeveloped.

The driving park was constructed by Walter T. Robbins, whose residence was where the "law office shingle" of my brother and I hangs today. The driving park, also referred to as the Trotting Park and later the old athletic association grounds, occupied the ancestral lands of the Robbins family. David Robbins settled on the property in 1740, the year of Leominster's incorporation, and his house still stands at the intersection of North Main Street and Hammond Streets. Walter Robbins was David's great-grandson. The driving park was, for many years, the center of Leominster entertainment. Residents gathered to wager on horse races, attend cattle shows, and watch and play baseball. Football came to the driving park in the early 1890s, and by October 20, 1894, the venerable old field hosted the first Leominster-Fitchburg football game.

When Bernard Doyle set out to assemble the land for Leominster's new athletic plant, the city already owned most of what was left of Robbins's Park. Doyle formed a committee that included Middlemas, John M. McPhee, and Bertram H. Hayes to acquire the target properties. In March of 1929, Middlemas began the process of negotiating purchase contracts with the various landowners. The work was long and arduous. The task required travel to New York several times, as well as trips to Baltimore, Newton, Medford, and Jamaica Plain. He spent two months communicating with the representatives of one land owner in Huntington, West Virginia.

On Saturday, March 8, 1930, the *Fitchburg Sentinel* reported an announcement by Raymond Middlemas that the entire twenty-acre site had been acquired. The land included three homes on Revere Street, which was discontinued with other streets within the parcel on May 26, 1930. The homes were eventually moved off the site to nearby Grand Street. The landscape architect, Herbert J. Kelloway, expected work to begin in April and, weather permitting, the high school football field to be ready in late September.

The large-scale excavation and field construction project attracted twelve bidders. The committee awarded the contract to a Leominster firm, Tragia Construction Company. The contract was made public on June 4, 1930. On the same day, Frank Tragia walked the site and watched as his steam shovel and trucks began the process of removing the earth, following the careful specifications and Mr. Kelloway's plan.

Tragia planned to mobilize additional steam shovels and trucks soon. The scope of work was daunting. His company reportedly moved 25,000 cubic yards of earth and imported 16,000 cubic yards of loam for the new fields. The supply of loam became a problem. The committee supplied Tragia with material it obtained from the city at no cost. Loam was moved from street-widening projects at Highland Avenue and Nashua Street. The material proved to be inadequate, as it was contaminated with stones, roots, and debris. When Tragia protested, Middlemas bought some more land. The committee acquired the fourteen-acre Burchstead farm on Nashua Street and stripped more than ten thousand cubic yards of its high-quality farm loam, which covered the inferior material once the rubbish was removed. The new loamed surfaces were sown with six tons of grass seed and enriched with fifteen tons of bone meal.

Football was not played at the new field in the fall of 1930. The moving of the three homes on Revere Street, discontinuance by the city of five streets, and the bidding process delayed the project more than two months. The architect's projection was overly optimistic. The Leominster football warriors would have to wait until the 1931 season before football was played at the new field.

On Monday evening, April 27, 1931, former Mayor Bernard F. Doyle formally gifted Doyle Field by deed to the City of Leominster. The city council, authorized by a special act of the Massachusetts legislature that permitted the acceptance of the gift and established a commission to maintain the field, voted to accept the gift. The vision Bernard Doyle shared with Raymond Middlemas more than two years before had moved from thought to reality. The rains of that spring would fall quietly on a new landscape that replaced a barren, overgrown wasteland. The field house, complete with locker rooms, showers, and a ticket office, was still under construction. As the 1931 construction season brought accomplishment of the final details, attention turned to a dedication ceremony and football at Doyle Field.

Coach Raymond C. Comerford was eager to lead his football team onto Doyle Field. The Doyle Field committee had consulted Coach Comerford on a number of occasions regarding construction of the athletic facility and field house. Comerford became Leominster's football coach in the 1927 season. In his first season, Leominster was defeated by Fitchburg by a score of 64–0. The defeat was humiliating. It still represents the largest scoring disparity in the long series between the two teams. Leominster had traveled to Fitchburg's Crocker Field each year since 1918 and had come home with only a tie (1921, 7–7) and one victory (1925, 9–0) through the 1927 season. Neither the trend nor the lack of a home venue were lost on the new coach or Mayor Doyle. Coach Comerford was well liked and determined. Trips to Crocker Field on Thanksgiving in 1928 and 1929 resulted in Leominster victories by scores of 6–3 and 6–0, respectively.

The 1928 victory earned Leominster its first award of the Nicholson Cup. Named for its donor, Haldie Nicholson, the silver cup is a prize still awarded annually to the winner of the Thanksgiving game to retain for the ensuing year. Mr. Nicholson thought the beautiful trophy would be an extra incentive for the rival squads. An English immigrant who came to pursue the manufacture of umbrella handles and other novelties from horn, he was intensely supportive of high school athletics. When he died on October 20, 1934 (ironically, the fortieth anniversary of the "first" Leominster-Fitchburg game), the entire LHS football team attended his funeral. The first award of the Nicholson Cup occurred on Thanksgiving, 1926. The silver cup was hoisted by FHS Captain Danny Quinn, who was carried about Crocker Field in celebration. At a banquet for the FHS football team, Alvah Crocker and Leominster's mayor, Bernard Doyle, made a formal presentation of the cup to the winners. Given the history of the rivalry during the 1920s, the wins Leominster achieved in those last two seasons of the decade were significant achievements.

As the new decade of the 1930s started, Leominster supporters looked forward to a new field and a greater competitiveness. In August of 1930, Leominster's Coach Comerford traveled to the University of Illinois to attend a three-week program at Coach "Pop" Warner's football school. Leominster had lost many veteran players to graduation in 1930, including its entire starting backfield. The coach was intent to put the best team on the field. Comerford succeeded in building a strong Leominster team. Entering the climactic Thanksgiving game with Fitchburg, his team would lose only one game, to Amesbury High School, by a score of 7–0. The Leominster team, led by a stalwart defense, entered its game with Fitchburg outscoring its opponents

91–9. The Leominster defense shut out six opponents and, in addition to the Amesbury loss, permitted Gardner a safety in a 13–2 victory over the Chair City eleven.

Success was no stranger to the Red and Gray either. Fitchburg outscored its opponents 234–33. Like the Blue and White, FHS lost only one game, to powerful Brockton, 20–13. All of Fitchburg's ten victories were shutouts, except a 33–13 win over St. John's High School. The match with Leominster was greatly anticipated. The strength of the teams, the construction of Leominster's new field, and a new found yearning to claim the coveted Nicholson Cup heightened excitement for the annual classic.

The crowd filed into Crocker Field on Thursday, November 27, 1930. Mark O'Toole fastened his coat against the brisk November air. Memories flooded his mind. Comparisons were inescapable. The crowd was enormous. Estimates placed the total admittance at eight thousand, the largest ever to witness a Fitchburg-Leominster game. When O'Toole lined up against Fitchburg at the old trotting park in 1894 for the very first meeting of the rivals, the crowd numbered only a few hundred. He now watched the immense crowd, in a sea of school colors, gathered around a modern Crocker Field. His pride swelled as his two oldest sons ran onto the field. David O'Toole, a senior and class president, was Leominster's starting left end. Richard, a sophomore, was the backup quarterback.[81]

Leominster lost a thrilling, hard-fought game, 6–0. Both O'Toole boys figured in the play. Starting quarterback Frank McCann was injured the Saturday before Thanksgiving and played sparingly, mostly on passing plays. Richard O'Toole backed up McCann, doing an admirable job in the important game. David O'Toole caught a critical pass and carried the ball to the Fitchburg two-yard line. Both defenses made a number of goal-line stands and, unfortunately for Leominster,

---

81　Mark and Mary O'Toole had seven children: Mary E., Anna E., David L., Richard J., Mark K., Edward B., and Jane C. Mark K. O'Toole was also a Leominster High School gridder who was commissioned a lieutenant in World War II. He was killed in action in 1943 when the plane he piloted crashed.

the opportunity created by O'Toole's reception was one of them. The headlines said it all:

Fitchburg High Is Victor
In Thrilling Grid Classic

8000 See Sensational Struggle Between Leominster and Red and Gray; Lateral Contributes To Only Touchdown; Both Teams Threaten Frequently; Dyer and McCann, Crippled, Give Remarkable Exhibition; Comb City Boys Get 11 First Downs, Fitchburg 8

Fitchburg high crossed the Leominster high goal line in the second period yesterday morning at Crocker Field for the first time since 1927 and that lone touchdown was sufficient to win the annual classic from Leominster High, 6 to 0. Leominster failed to score on Fitchburg, thus duplicating the score of last year but reversing the teams.

It was a game of thrills and spectacular play. Both teams emerged from the contest covered with glory.

It was a battle of evenly matched, superbly coached football teams and Fitchburg won by means of a 25-yard run at the end of a lateral pass which proved to be effective all season.

The lonesome touchdown came after Leominster had held Fitchburg twice within the five-yard line and once inside the 15-yard line, showing that the Red and Gray had four scoring chances before being able to make the opportunities count.[82]

No one, including Mark O'Toole, veteran of that very first struggle, came away without a great respect for the effort of both teams, their respective coaches, or the caliber of the rivalry between the two schools.

---

82 *Fitchburg Sentinel,* November 28, 1930.

Later that afternoon, Mark O'Toole borrowed a friend's automobile to take his daughter Mary back to Wellesley College. On his way home, O'Toole was stricken ill upon reaching Littleton about 4:30 PM. He was found dead at the wheel of the car, having succumbed to a heart attack. The fact that the automobile belonged to Edward Lawless caused confusion as to the identity of the deceased, it being surmised initially that Mr. Lawless had died. O'Toole was fifty-two, and, like his father before him, passed away far too young. He left a widow and children ranging in age from Mary, who was eighteen, to his youngest, Jane, who was five. St. Leo's Church was filled with mourners, and Mayor Platt closed city hall during the services. A delegation of the schoolmates of David and Richard came to the church as a group, and former Mayor Bernard Doyle and Raymond Middlemas were among the pallbearers.

Mark O'Toole's death quickly changed the perspective on the Thanksgiving football game of 1930. Nevertheless, the ebb and flow of life would continue. Despite the loss of a respected friend and citizen, the living would look ahead—O'Toole would not have wanted it any other way. Unfortunately, tragedy would strike Leominster's football community again before Doyle Field could host its long-awaited first game.

Football seasons come and go, some with greater notoriety for their achievements or disappointments. As August begins to yield a few cooler evenings, the focus shifts to football. Anticipation of autumn and football was never greater in Leominster than in 1931. Coach Comerford aspired to continue and build upon the success of the prior season. Winning would be the very best way to inaugurate the spectacular new Doyle Field. On August 24, Dr. Alfred A. Wheeler began physical examinations of the 1931 Leominster football candidates. Coach Comerford scheduled practices to start the last week of August. School was scheduled to open September 9, and the team would face its first opponent, Nashua High School, on September 19.

Before the rigors of the new football season got underway, Ray Comerford traveled to Sunset Beach near Manchester, Massachusetts. Manchester was just a bit more than thirty miles from his hometown of West Roxbury. The coach relaxed in the sun and felt the gentle breezes of the Atlantic. Suddenly, the natural sounds of wind and

121

surf were pierced by the cries of a young boy struggling against the waves. Instinctively, the coach plunged in the sea and swam feverishly to the boy. He reached the young lad and began the laborious task of swimming to shore with the extra load. Before long, the thirty-year-old coach tired and called for help. Two men reached the pair; one aided the young boy, and the other assisted Comerford. Comerford's rescuer could not hold him against a crashing wave that separated them. The boy was saved. Coach Comerford was not.

Raymond Comerford's body was found at 5:30 AM the following day, a half mile from where he was last seen. The newspaper reported his death on Wednesday, August 26, the same day the body was recovered. The community was devastated by the loss of a man who had gained so many friends and earned the respect of the boys he trained and all of Leominster's residents. Comerford, who also served as Leominster athletic director, gave the Leominster football a stability it had not previously enjoyed in the past when coaching duties often shifted each season.

A 1925 graduate of Dartmouth, Coach Comerford was a smallish, retiring man, often quiet and never brash. He was a great teacher of the game who commanded respect and attention while reaping devotion. His teams believed in him and "his shy tight-lipped grin, and the pleased expression in the eyes behind his heavy glasses as he meted out small praise, was reward enough for any LHS athletes."[83] He lived alone at 34 Cotton Street in Leominster and was survived by five brothers all residing in his native West Roxbury, where he was waked in his family home. His funeral and burial were at Holy Name Parish in Roxbury. Hundreds of Leominster residents, including a group consisting of seventy-five young Leominster athletes, attended both his wake and funeral. Among the mourners were Bernard Doyle and Raymond Middlemas, whose interest in Leominster athletics had drawn them close to the coach. Coach Comerford would never coach a team on the turf of Doyle Field; however, his contribution to Leominster football would not be forgotten. The *Fitchburg Sentinel*, with just a few words, captured the essence of it all. "He died as he lived, aiding the younger."[84]

---

83 *Fitchburg Sentinel*, August 26, 1931.
84 *Fitchburg Sentinel*, August 26, 1931.

Once again, the Leominster football community would have to persevere. Assistant Coach Walter Deacon started practice as scheduled, and the search for a new director of physical education and football began in earnest. The leading candidate recommended unanimously by the athletic council to the school committee was Charles Broderick, a New Hampshire native and coach of the successful Amesbury High School football team, the only team to defeat LHS in 1930. Despite the ringing endorsement, at least two members of the school committee, Clarence M. Joyce and Dr. I.W. Smith, had reservations about the fast-track selection of Broderick. A quick decision needed to be made in fairness to Amesbury and for the better of the Leominster program. Broderick was hired and began by far the longest tenure of a Leominster head football coach.

Like Coach Comerford before him, Broderick's first season was not his most memorable, at least in pure football terms. His first game as Leominster's football coach was played before a crowd of two thousand, squeezed into the tight confines of the athletic field behind the high school in a cold drizzle. The Dean Academy second team spoiled Broderick's debut, defeating Leominster 6–0 on Saturday, September 26, 1931. It was the last football game that the Blue and White would play on the mud-soaked field, a field that Fitchburg High refused to ever play on. In less than two weeks, the LHS eleven would move from the substandard, oversized sandlot to one of the greatest high school fields in the country. Leominster anxiously anticipated the opening of its new recreation facility.

Dedication day came on Saturday, October 10, 1931. A day of activities began that morning with a track meet and a baseball game that pitted teams from two of Leominster's largest factories, Whitney Carriage Company and DuPont-Viscoloid Company. As the October sunshine warmed the large open spaces that afternoon, a crowd gathered to witness the historic ceremony of the field's presentation and acceptance. The program included an impressive array of political leaders and dignitaries. More importantly, Leominster's citizens from all walks of life, young and old, athletes, budding and aging, turned out to show Mr. Doyle their appreciation. Seated at the speaker's platform was a man contented to observe. The quiet guest had spent the last thirty years living on Pine Street, just a few blocks from the new field. Memories collected over many decades filtered through his mind as an undeniable sense of pride filled him. Bernard W. Doyle Sr. could choose among numerous accomplishments in defining his son's triumphs; however, October 10 was special. The day was a perfect manifestation of well-directed success, the kind of gesture that earns a father's esteem.

The speakers recognized the donor, the Doyle Field Committee, especially Mr. Middlemas, and a number of other contributors to the project. Secretary to the newly formed Doyle Field Commission Judge J. Warren Healey recognized the input of Coach Louis Little, Leominster's very own, whose fame was destined to grow in a short few years, as well as the spirit of Coach Comerford, who tragically never witnessed the opening of the field he so eagerly anticipated. Judge Healey recognized a few of Leominster's recent gridiron stars who were in attendance, including James Barrett, captain of Harvard's 1929 football team, who was the victim of the legendary tooth punch out in the 1923 LHS-FHS basketball game.

The last two speakers delivered the "Dedicatory Addresses." The speakers were the Honorable Marcus A. Coolidge and the Honorable David I. Walsh, both Massachusetts incumbent United States senators. Remarkably, the assembled crowd claimed a prideful connection to both men, since Senator Walsh was born in Leominster and Senator Coolidge was educated in Leominster schools. Senator Walsh concluded the dedication program with the following:

> Leominster today congratulates the most generous and public-spirited citizen—one whose life from humble beginnings through struggle and perseverance to a position of enormous security, so splendidly typifies the equality of opportunities that America more than any other nation in the world bequeaths to her sons.

Bernard W. Doyle understood the opportunities America bestowed and the best evidence of that knowledge is what he gave back to his native city, a place he loved. His words that day captured his sense of it all.

Every man, I think, has a natural love for the place of his birth, for his friends and associates of a lifetime. I am no exception. I have a great love of this beautiful City of Leominster, for its people, and for its institutions.

Athletic sports have always been of great interest to me. I believe that recreation and sports have a proper and necessary place in the education of youth and in the development of both character and physique. I also believe that wholesome sport for all ages and classes of people is good for a community. I have long realized the need of proper recreational facilities in this city.

Prompted by these thoughts and feelings, this recreation field has been developed. It is with great satisfaction that I now present to our Honorable Mayor, the representative of the people of Leominster, the deeds formally transferring this athletic field to the City of Leominster. It is my hope that the field will be of the greatest possible enjoyment to all the people of this city.[85]

The first football game on Doyle Field was played on Columbus Day, Monday, October 12, 1931. The *Fitchburg Sentinel* reported, "Upsetting the time honored custom of losing the first game on a new field, Leominster High defeated Rogers High of Newport, R.I. 14–12 on Doyle Field yesterday morning before a crowd of close to 5,000 spectators."[86] Coach Broderick's success was short lived in 1931. LaSalle Academy visited on Saturday, October 17, handing the home team a 25–0 loss, the first suffered on Doyle Field. On Saturday, October 24, Amesbury came to town. Amesbury boys presented the former coach with a gold chain and pocket knife at Doyle Field's fifty-yard line just before the action got underway and a 12–7 defeat when it was over.

October drew to a close, and Leominster's police chief, J.H. Mead, augmented his police squad by appointing several reserves as the city prepared for the annual perambulations of ghosts and goblins; it didn't work, as several homes and automobiles suffered broken windows.

---

85 *Fitchburg Sentinel*, October 10, 1931.
86 *Fitchburg Sentinel*, October 13, 1931.

Trouble of another sort plagued the maiden season of Coach Broderick. By October 29, the Leominster team was in a state of chaos. The team posted a dismal 1–3 record, and the results were not acceptable to a community whose excitement was heightened by the opening of Doyle Field. A subtle but unmistakable undercurrent of discontent ran through Leominster, and the focus was the new coach. The spirit of the football players was sapped by the adults who were out to embarrass Broderick.

On the morning of October 29, the coach struck back in the newspaper and on the practice field. Leominster got its first taste of "C.B.," as he was affectionately known in later years. In an unequivocal and stingingly direct statement, the coach spoke to the *Leominster Enterprise*:

> There is no room for any 90 per centers on this squad. If the boys are not out here to fight with their team 100 per cent they can just turn in their suits and consider their athletic career at Leominster High School at an end. I am here to put a football team on the field and if the boys in the high school are not loyal enough to give me their support we'll have a team just the same. I'll put on a team if I have to go down to the Junior High School for material and play before a crowd of nine men and a police officer. I am here to put out a team and if any civilians who are not satisfied and are not man enough to come to me personally and register their complaint let them hold their peace and not poison the minds of a group of School boys to lie down on their school, their city and their own decency and self-respect. I am here to coach this team in my own way. I was hired to put a group of football players on the field but I cannot do it unless I get 100 per cent cooperation. I would rather have a dozen dubs that were playing with all they had than a group of temperamental athletes who are not out to fight all the time. I am going through with my contract to give this

school the best coaching I can, regardless of any adverse pressure or sore-headed friction.[87]

The practice that Broderick conducted the day before the newspaper announcement was of a completely different tempo. The *Leominster Enterprise* account used the adjective "snappy." The team held a scrimmage on the high school athletic field "with pep and precision … the boys were working hard out there all the time." A different attitude pervaded Leominster football, and the city got its first taste of a single-minded Charlie Broderick.

The results were almost immediate. The team traveled to Framingham to play a strong team from that city. Earlier that season, a strong Fitchburg squad was fortunate to tie Framingham 12–12 as a result of a late touchdown, when a twenty-five-yard penalty was imposed against Framingham, placing the ball on the Framingham five-yard line. The Blue and White warriors lost the game 13–6; however, it was clear that Leominster was playing a new brand of football. Leominster played Framingham well, and the outcome was in doubt for nearly the entire game. To put the achievement in a better perspective, Fitchburg was 7–1–1 in the nine games played before Thanksgiving, with only twenty-four points scored against the Red and Gray. Framingham scored twelve against Fitchburg in the tie, Brockton beat Fitchburg 6–0, and the remaining six points were scored by an Athol team that was dominated by Fitchburg 39–6. The Blue and White had amazed their fans with their performance against Framingham.

Leominster built upon its new found vigor, trouncing Clinton 41–0 on Saturday, November 7 at Doyle Field. Broderick paid homage to Coach Rockne's "Notre Dame System" when in the second period he inserted an entirely new and fresh offensive team into the game. Mark O'Toole's son, Dick, the enthusiastic quarterback of the second team, and other underclassmen gained some valuable experience in the process. Leominster's last game before its all-important Thanksgiving meeting with Fitchburg was played in Gardner against the Chair City team before a crowd of three thousand. Leominster triumphed by a score of 12–0. The Blue and White's offensive attack featured the slick play of 129-pound left halfback Ronald Cahill, who gained yards with

---

87   *Leominster Enterprise*, October 29, 1931.

his passes and runs. The three games played after the "realignment" spoke volumes about Broderick's coaching style and the future of Leominster's football program. There were hints of things to come, but first, Leominster looked forward to hosting the mighty Red and Gray at Doyle Field for the first time on Thanksgiving Day, 1931. Fitchburg had not played a Thanksgiving Day game in Leominster since 1917, when the visitors dominated the Leominsters 44–0.

Coach Amiott of Fitchburg and his Leominster counterpart, Charles Broderick, were not the only men planning for Thanksgiving. Leominster Police Chief John H. Mead spent days preparing for the expected record crowd. He assigned all available Leominster police officers, as well as a number of state police troopers, to duty. Thirty-two officers were deployed inside Doyle Field, and an additional twenty officers and troopers were used outside the field for traffic control, including motorcycle officer Raymond J. Matthews, who escorted the FHS team to and from Doyle Field. The newspapers were full of articles documenting the teams' preparations.

Leominster conducted its last scrimmage six days before Thanksgiving and held only light workouts thereafter. The coach wanted his squad in top form, especially the boys who were nursing minor injuries. Coach Amiott scrimmaged his team against a group of "ineligibles" on the Monday before the game and held a light workout the following day. The *Fitchburg Sentinel* reported the practice sessions and other details of the upcoming game, including a list of the results from prior years, which commenced with Fitchburg's 1895 victory by a score of 14–0 *and not the Leominster win of 40–0 in 1894.*

Fitchburg did not practice on Wednesday. The squad attended a rally at the high school and reconvened at the Crocker Field Club House at 7:00 PM. The players were entertained by a display of the hunting and fishing photos of local sportsman W. W. Putnam II. A more timely exhibition featured George Bergroth's motion picture of the 1930 Leominster-Fitchburg Thanksgiving game. The boys went home early to get their sleep. All were eager to earn their first victory on Doyle Field.

Finally, the gates of Doyle Field were opened, welcoming Fitchburg to the new stadium for the first time. The city's pride in its new "recreational plant" was a partial salve for the gloom cast over the nation that year. The market crash of 1929 had pushed America and the world into the Great Depression. As 1931 came to a close, the nation's unemployment ranks swelled to nine million, bank failures numbered more than two thousand, and those with jobs in many instances suffered wage cuts. The dire events did not dampen the spirit of the football fans who filed into Doyle Field on Thanksgiving Day 1931.

A record-breaking crowd of ten thousand came to see the Blue and White warriors battle the vaunted Red and Gray. The stands were filled to capacity, and the overflow crowd ringed the embankments of the new bowl, creating one unbroken oval throng of humanity and color. Just before 10:00 AM, Leominster Captain Eddie Tellier strode to midfield. It was a cold morning. Tellier won the coin toss, and with it, the first possession of the game for his team. On the very first play from scrimmage, Cahill threw a long pass to Pennery, which he just missed. Broderick was not afraid to make decisions or call an aggressive game. For much of the first period, the teams exchanged punts, including a sixty-three-yarder by Cahill that pinned Fitchburg on its own one-yard line. As the first period drew to a close, Leominster sustained a drive. The *Leominster Enterprise* captured the mood of the Leominster faithful:

> First to the heights of their fighting courage, inspired by the school spirit that fairly surcharged the atmosphere, the Leominster delegation fought like the consecrated zealots they were. Showing an offensive power and a drive that surprised even their most optimistic followers they crashed the ball down the field to score the first touchdown in the first play of the second period.[88]

The conversion was good, and Leominster laid claim to the first score and a 7–0 lead. Fitchburg scored next. The conversion attempt failed, and Leominster led the game 7–6. That score and the Leominster lead would stand through three quarters of play. The fourth period brought the turning point. Fitchburg, taking advantage of good field position, drove for a score but failed to make the extra points. The score

---

88   *Leominster Enterprise*, November 27, 1931.

stood Fitchburg 12, Leominster 7. Leominster had its turn. Under immense pressure, the scrambling Cahill attempted another long pass to Pennery, and the receiver made, in the words of the *Leominster Enterprise* reporter, "A Tris Speaker catch." Pennery picked up yards after the catch and carried the ball to the Fitchburg twenty-three-yard line. The Fitchburg fans gasped at the turn of events. A Leominster victory was not fairly conceivable, and the missed extra points were looming in the minds of the Red and Gray supporters.

As quickly as the Pennery pass reception advanced the ball, fortune turned. Tellier ripped a seven-yard run, fighting for every extra inch. In a cruel twist, Tellier's extra effort prolonged the play long enough for the ball to be jarred loose, and Fitchburg's Bill Whalen recovered. Fitchburg's defense made a play, and now the offense would have another opportunity. The Red and Gray's left halfback had his ribs wrapped in an adhesive cast. The 150-pound Milton Savitt needed a cushion to protect himself against further injury and the inevitable pain from a day of jarring tackles. Savitt was Fitchburg's workhorse that day. He was focused and eagerly awaited each carry of the pigskin.

The Fitchburg offense lined up at the spot of Tellier's fumble, its own eighteen-yard line. The Red and Gray once again looked to Savitt. The talented back powered through a hole, opened at Leominster's right end, and picked up a downfield block as Paavo Lahti took out Pennery. Savitt's run turned quickly to an unimpeded sprint. He couldn't feel his ribs as he crossed the Leominster goal, capping the eighty-two-yard scamper and dashing Leominster's hopes. The mood on each side of the field could not have been more different. With the game out of hand and the clock nearing expiration, each team freely substituted, enabling the bench the distinction of having played in the holiday classic. The final score of the day came when backup quarterback Kenneth Killay had his pass intercepted by Fitchburg's backup Everett Daulton, who ran it back for a touchdown.

The final score, Fitchburg 24, Leominster 7, did not reflect the nature of the competition. The home crowd had hoped for a different result, a different first clash with Fitchburg at Doyle Field. Despite the outcome, their team battled honorably. The *Leominster Enterprise* byline in the prose of the day doffed its cap. "After giving their full measure of true blue devotion, they were carried off on their shields, after an overpowering Red and Gray surge had breathed a fell blast in their forces in the fourth period of a conflict as spectacular and thrill-packed as any that had marked the long feud between the two rival camps."[89] The Blue and White that took the field that Thanksgiving was a team that differed dramatically from the Leominster eleven that began the season. The year had witnessed a remarkable number of changes and after the tragic loss of Coach Raymond Comerford, the emergence of Charles Broderick. The new coach had placed his stamp on Leominster football. No one knew exactly what lay ahead, but it was evident that the new coach was a fighter and the rivalry was alive and well.

---

89   *Leominster Enterprise*, November 27, 1931.

—— Chapter Eleven ——

Noteworthy Seasons and Games to Remember

One hundred and fourteen seasons have passed. The long history of the rivalry has produced a number of memorable contests and legendary teams. Some games and teams come readily to the contemporary mind, and others are buried in fading newspaper clippings and high school yearbooks. Recollections from those seasons gone by no longer echo, and the players who roamed the early gridirons are gone.

Attempting to hand-pick a few games and seasons from more than eleven decades of football is a difficult task that involves a great deal of editorial judgment. What follows should not be considered anything more than one solitary attempt to impart a handful of compelling stories. These accounts deserve to be retold; however, the list does not and should not represent an exclusive tally of the most significant points along the way of the long history between the two schools. On the contrary, what breathes life into this old rivalry is the notion that there is but one constant, the yearning to compete. The history resulting from the rivalry is ever mutable. The story changes with the passage of time, each generation and new edition. That said, the following contests and seasons should not be forgotten.

Thursday, November 27, 1913, Coach Amiott's First Season

On a night when the temperature dipped to ten degrees below zero, more than eight hundred people assembled at Fitchburg High School to honor longtime Fitchburg Director of Athletics and beloved Coach Clarence N. Amiott. The testimonial held on the evening of January 18, 1938 commemorated the retirement of Coach Amiott after twenty-five years of service to Fitchburg High School athletics. Despite his quarter-century tenure, Amiott was only forty-eight when he was forced to retire as a result of a heart ailment that took his life nearly five years later on November 11, 1942.

Coach Amiott's career at Fitchburg High School was a thing of legend. As a basketball coach, Amiott led FHS to 310 victories in 401 games played, a .775 winning percentage, including a national championship in 1926. On the gridiron, Amiott helped the Red and Gray earn 173 victories in 252 games for a winning percentage of .724. Amiott was loved by his athletes, one hundred of which followed his example into coaching careers of their own.

The celebration honoring Amiott's career included an alumni basketball game, a speaking program that featured Arthur Sampson of the *Boston Herald* and "Swede" Nelson of Harvard, and movies. The program concluded with a presentation to the coach of twenty-five silver dollars and a check for $600, half the price of a 1939 Packard. Mayor Woollacott presented him with a bouquet of roses.

Clarence Noah Amiott was a 1911 graduate of Fitchburg High School. A well-liked student athlete, "Noey," as his classmates nicknamed him, was the captain of both the football and basketball teams. The class yearbook deemed "A Mighty Hercules Was He." Just two years out of high school, Amiott became Fitchburg High School's director of athletics and football coach in June of 1913. With his appointment, the fortunes of Fitchburg football were forever changed.

When Coach Amiott took charge of Fitchburg's football team, the more recent success belonged to Leominster High School. Of the six games played from 1910 to 1912, LHS had won five, and the sixth contest resulted in a scoreless tie. Amiott meant to change that trend. The first game played in 1913 also ended in a scoreless tie. Fitchburg's chance to stem the tide came on Thanksgiving Day, November 27, 1913. Two thousand fans invaded the Circle Street grounds. The newspaper remarked that sixteen electric trolley cars were needed to handle the transportation of the crowd.

Amiott had his team prepared. FHS played a "grand game." According to the *Fitchburg Sentinel,* "There were many brilliant plays and players but it was the consistent, persistent and all together work of the entire squad that enabled Fitchburg to emerge from the day with the laurels and victory crowning one of the most successful seasons every enjoyed."[90] Fitchburg's cheerleaders "kept up a constant storm of cheers, songs and yells" while Officer Charles Donovan and nine other officers, two on horseback, maintained civil order. Left end Rogal made the play of the game when a Leominster punt was blocked by Fitchburg's guard Herndon near midfield. Rogal scooped up the loose ball and rambled fifty-five yards on route to Fitchburg's second touchdown and a 13–0 lead, which held up as the final score. With victory assured, Coach Amiott was able to play all of his senior players in their last high school game. Amid clanging bells, blowing horns, and banging drums, the Fitchburg fans celebrated their first Thanksgiving victory since 1909. If Fitchburg football had a different feel in November of 1913, then those sensing that were reading the pulse correctly. Fitchburg High School would reel off eleven straight victories after the Thanksgiving 1913 contest. Amiott would coach in twenty-eight Leominster-Fitchburg games, earning twenty wins and two ties. The 1913 games launched a great career that contributed some of the most memorable games of the rivalry. Clarence N. Amiott's devotion to Fitchburg athletics and football fueled the flame of competition between his alma mater and its traditional foe. Coach Amiott will always hold an important place in the history of Fitchburg-Leominster football.

Fitchburg High School 1924

By 1924, Coach Clarence Amiott had built a series of powerful teams that not only dominated neighbor Leominster High School but also provided stiff competition to several tough eastern Massachusetts football programs. The Fitchburg eleven faced ten opponents in 1924

---

90   *Fitchburg Sentinel,* November 28, 1913.

and won eight of the contests. The two losses came at the hands of powerful teams from Brockton and Waltham. Despite their defeats, the season was one of the most remarkable ever played by a Fitchburg team.

On Wednesday, October 29, twenty-one Fitchburg High School players boarded a train bound for Maywood, Illinois, with the rousing support of their fellow students. The boys were traveling west to take on Proviso High School, one of the most powerful football programs in the nation. The challenge was magnified by two prior meetings of the teams. Fitchburg lost at Proviso in 1922 and again in 1923 when the Red and Gray hosted the Midwest powerhouse.

The 1924 game was different. The Fitchburg team, led by quarterback Johnny Dillon, beat the Proviso team by a score of 20–6 on Saturday, November 2, 1924. Left halfback Leo Boudreau scored two touchdowns, and right halfback Walter Sullivan added a third. Some of the sportswriters of the day considered the game nothing short of a national championship.

The victorious Fitchburg football team was treated to a White House visit on their way back to Fitchburg and was warmly greeted by President and Massachusetts native Calvin Coolidge. When the train finally returned to Fitchburg's depot the following Tuesday, the victors were treated to a celebration they never forgot. The *Fitchburg Sentinel* captured the excitement on Tuesday, November 4, 1924:

> Much as a conquering king and his coterie were welcomed in the days of heraldry, Fitchburg High School's intrepid warriors returned home from a glorious victory. The victorious youths were escorted through the streets of the city amid frantic cheers, excited dances and happy laughter of their fellow pupils, to whom they are today the heroes.
>
> Fitchburg's boys won and today the city is theirs. The happiness of the victor is not confined to the high school. There is joy in nearly every home because of their wonderful achievement.[91]

---

91   *Fitchburg Sentinel*, November 4, 1924.

The remarkable achievement of victory over Proviso was not the last notable event of the season. On November 27, 1924, Thanksgiving Day, the Fitchburg and Leominster High School football teams renewed their rivalry. The 1923 edition of "the game" was not played because a Fitchburg player named Erwin Beach punched out the front teeth of Leominster's James "Red" Barrett during a basketball game at the Leominster High School gymnasium in the spring of 1923. Fitchburg severed athletic relations with Leominster after Leominster High's principal questioned Beach's eligibility to play in a basketball tournament after the incident. Apparently, the Leominster school official had not taken into account the "one free slug per season" rule in basketball! The *Fitchburg Sentinel's* post-game coverage noted that Beach, a burly left tackle and member of Fitchburg's class of 1923, got a rousing ovation when he entered Crocker Field accompanied by former Fitchburg player and quarterback Larry Hobbs as spectators for the 1924 Thanksgiving game with Leominster.

The *Fitchburg Sentinel* headline of November 28 summed up the game succinctly: "Fitchburg Crushes Leominster 48-0." Leominster didn't manage a single first down against the Fitchburg starters. In 1925, the Leominster High School boys earned a 9–0 victory over Fitchburg, its first in thirteen years, and some sorely needed tonic for the health of a rivalry that would never be interrupted again.

Leominster's 1932 Season

It did not take Coach Charles Broderick long to convert his doubters. Before too much of the 1932 season had passed, the near mutiny and undercurrents that the new coach had faced in 1931 were already in the distant past. The '32 team had a number of talented and experienced players who returned from the prior season. Among those were Richard O'Toole, Eddie Tellier, and Ronald Cahill. O'Toole, who successfully quarterbacked the 1932 team, was the son of Mark O'Toole, who played in the first Leominster-Fitchburg game in 1894. Mark O'Toole, who died at age fifty on Thanksgiving Day, 1930, would not get to see his son Richard's exploits in 1932.[92]

---

92   Three successive generations followed Mark O'Toole onto the grid-iron for Leominster High School. O'Toole's sons, David, class of

The Leominster team of 1932 was a solid, talented, and well-coached squad. The team still ranks as one of the most, if not *the* most, dominant ever fielded by the Blue and White. Leominster outscored its opponents by a remarkable 205–12 on its way to an unbeaten season. Only two opponents achieved scores against LHS in 1932: Concord in an LHS 41–6 victory and Gardner in the closest contest won by Leominster, 14–6.

The Leominster team gathered by the bus for the trip to Fitchburg on Thanksgiving morning in 1932. Coach Broderick paced back and forth—Ronnie Cahill was nowhere to be found. The team could not leave without Cahill, still a junior; he was just too good. When he finally arrived a half hour late (the left halfback had been hunting that morning), Broderick kept his cool, not only because of the young man's value to the team, but probably in deference to the humble attitude the young star always maintained.

When they finally got there, Leominster earned a resounding victory at Crocker Field. The Leominster backfield combination of O'Toole, Cahill, Tellier, and Gardner worked methodically and with devastating effect. O'Toole quarterbacked the team with a smooth efficiency, and Cahill was a legendary triple threat, running, punting, and tossing precise passes over the heads of Fitchburg defenders. Tellier slashed the Fitchburg line being led by blocking back Jimmy Gardner, the least-heralded of the quartet, who at season's end was elected the team's honorary captain for his solid play and team accomplishments. The ball was in Fitchburg's territory for much of the game, and the Red and Gray's offense could only accomplish but two first downs.

1931; Richard, class of 1933; and Mark, class of 1936, all played for Leominster. The youngest son, Mark K. O'Toole, an air force lieutenant, was killed in action during World War II. O'Toole's daughter, Jane, LHS Class of 1943, married Dr. John J. Curley's son, John J. Curley Jr., who played football for Leominster, graduating with the class of 1942. Two sons of John J. Curley Jr. played on the Leominster team: Michael, who graduated in 1973, and Daniel, who played on the Leominster undefeated team of 1974. Daniel graduated in 1977. Michael Curley's sons were fourth-generation Leominster football players. Mark O'Toole Curley, named for his great-grandfather, graduated in 2002, and Michael graduated in 2007.

Unbeknown to Coach Broderick, who disdained living in the shadow of Coach Comerford, the team dedicated the Thanksgiving game to their former coach, who tragically drowned just before the 1931 season started. Leominster's center in 1932, Riccardo "Rick" Cavaioli, became simply "Cavy" to Coach Comerford as a sophomore during the 1930 season. Sitting in his easy chair today with an alert vigor, "Cavy" recalls the man who gave him his nickname seventy-nine football seasons ago. On the practice field, Comerford sometimes strung together a slew of other names that crudely noted Cavaioli's Italian heritage. Once practice was over, though, the coach was a gentleman who would offer players a ride home, which was more than a simple gesture in 1930 when boys walked miles home from practice. The boys' achievement in 1932, not unlike other successful campaigns, was spurred by a feeling of "togetherness," as Cavaioli remembers it. The dedication to Comerford was even greater motivation.[93]

The final score, 25–0, represented Leominster's largest winning margin since the 1894 game when Leominster won 40–0. In 1932, the next-largest winning margin over Fitchburg belonged to the 1910 team, captained by the legendary Lou Little, which beat Fitchburg 23–0. Little, who coached Columbia football team from 1930 to 1956, attended a banquet given for Leominster's football heroes on Thursday evening, December 15, 1932 at city hall. Little himself knew a little about undefeated teams; the squad he captained in 1910 was the first LHS team to achieve that distinction.

Little's 1910 team met the FHS contingent at Leominster's old driving park before a crowd of six thousand and thrashed a Red and Gray eleven that was outweighed and outplayed. The rear of the huge crowd was ringed by automobiles parked in rows three deep, the horns of which rang out in chorus with cheers for the home team. After Leominster's third touchdown, the Fitchburg crowd broke through the rope and police line, causing a significant delay before order could be restored. The last Leominster score was followed by an even more regrettable incident when Noah Amiott, later Fitchburg's legendary coach, was assaulted and bloodied by frustrated Fitchburg rowdies when a play carried him out of bounds.

---

93   Personal interview with Riccardo Cavaioli, Friday, January 23, 2009.

When Little came to Leominster in December of 1932, thoughts of his 1910 team were not far from his mind:

> This gathering takes me back twenty-two years ago this month to a dinner given the Leominster high school 1910 football team. Rev. George Baker acted as toastmaster and the late Senator Blodgett gave the address. I see in this audience many faces who were there twenty-two years ago. You don't know how honored I was, as I sat there as the captain of that team. It is one of the most vivid recollections of my own playing days. I feel highly complimented to be invited here to pay my respects to this victorious team.
>
> Football is a great game for it brings together the entire community. All parties unite. That is what makes it what it is today. Remember football is not a new game; it dates back to 500 B.C.
>
> We read of miracle coaches, but in football there are no miracles performed. There are not "miracle coaches". You had a successful team because you had men in Coach Broderick and Coach Kucharski out there coaching you that knew their business. Your success was the result of good hard work.
>
> You had fine coaching and you learned your lesson well. That the players co-operated with the coaches is evident for it is one of the oldest axioms of football "as you practice so you will play." Football has changed since the good old days. It is no longer a game of brawn. It is not the old push haul. It is power, speed and deception. It is now the most scientific game.[94]

The 1932 season, like the one Little captained twenty-two years before, brought together a group of young men who believed in each other and, more importantly, in their team. The achievements of those years represent two of Leominster's five undefeated seasons. Four of the five undefeated teams had perfect records, being untied as well.

---

94 *Leominster Enterprise*, December 16, 1932.

The lone undefeated season that included a tie was 1952. Each of those five seasons has grown its own legend, all of them different, but, like the rivalry itself, sustained by the peculiar circumstances, diverse personalities, and unique sequence of play that gives each meeting between Fitchburg and Leominster it own distinct flavor. Each year, varying factors combine with a constant desire to compete, producing an ever-present yearn for the gridiron.

A Titanic Clash, 1933

President Franklin Delano Roosevelt was sworn in for the first of his four terms, and the initial months of his administration brought a dizzying array of acronyms describing agencies designed to lead America out of the Great Depression. A number of noteworthy gangsters were nearing the end of their infamous careers. John Dillinger, Bonnie and Clyde, "Pretty Boy" Floyd, and "Baby Face" Nelson were still mesmerizing America. All of those infamous villains would not be snared in the web of justice until the following year. In this climate of uncertainty, Leominster and Fitchburg would take to the gridiron in the autumn of 1933.

Both teams fielded powerful squads, each led by accomplished triple-threat backs: senior Ronnie Cahill for Leominster and senior Bill Mackie for Fitchburg. Each team had great success, and for the only time in the history of the rivalry, Thanksgiving was a battle of unbeatens. Fitchburg scored 287 points en route to besting ten opponents who mustered only thirty-four. In the last game before the holiday classic, the Red and Gray pasted Chicopee High School by a score of 60–0.

Leominster's record also demonstrated dominance. The Blue and White defeated all nine of their opponents, scoring 237 points. Leominster gave up only a single touchdown to Amesbury, Rogers High School, and Gardner, and one extra point, for a total of nineteen points allowed. Leominster's other six opponents were shut out, and, like Fitchburg, the Blue and White rolled into Thanksgiving on an impressive victory, beating Andover 41–0.

The stage was set unlike ever before: Leominster vs. Fitchburg; Cahill vs. Mackie. The game was recognized as the unofficial state championship. Thanksgiving arrived on the last day of November and brought fair skies and ideal weather. More than ten thousand spectators crowded into Doyle Field. It was the largest crowd ever to witness a Leominster-Fitchburg game. The game lived up to its billing.

Leominster threatened first. The Blue and White engineered a first-period drive, starting on its own twenty-five-yard line. Cahill ran and passed the ball to the Fitchburg ten-yard line. However, the Fitchburg defense held off Leominster, and the initial quarter ended without a score.

Fitchburg earned the only score of the first half when fullback Lauri Shattuck crossed into the middle of the Leominster secondary on a fourth-down play, catching a pass rifled by Mackie in stride at the Leominster fifteen-yard line. Shattuck high-stepped one Leominster defender and got a block on his way into the opponent's end zone standing up.

The second half started badly for Leominster when an unfocused kick-receiving team failed to cover the kick and instead let Fitchburg's S. Esielonis recover the ball at Leominster's thirty-two-yard line. Shattuck and Mackie slashed the Leominster line on repeated runs and scored the Red and Gray's second touchdown. The point after failed, and Fitchburg led 13–0. Leominster fought back with a scoring drive that featured a thirty-three-yard Cahill pass and several runs by the outstanding halfback, which culminated with a five-yard plunge for Leominster's first touchdown. Cahill missed the extra point, and the score stood at 13–6. Fitchburg added another touchdown on a Mackie run in the fourth period, followed by a Shattuck run for the extra point, and the lead was increased to 20–6. Leominster was running out of time. The Blue and White capitalized on a muffed punt by Fitchburg deep in its own territory when Cahill carried a Fitchburg defender into the end zone on a short run to Leominster's second touchdown. The score was too little and too late, and the thrilling contest ended with Fitchburg victorious by a final score of 20–12.

The *Fitchburg Sentinel's* headline recorded "Fitchburg High Triumphs in Sharply Fought Battle." Leominster notched thirteen first downs to Fitchburg's twelve, and the contest was crisply played with only a few scant penalties in one series of downs. The *Fitchburg Sentinel* summed up a classic, "Not only was victory at stake but also the rightful claim of the victors to the mythical state championship. When the final whistle sounded Fitchburg High had earned that right by defeating its traditional rival Leominster High 20–12 in a titanic battle."[95]

Dominance on the Gridiron and Conflict Abroad, 1952

The 1952 football campaigns for Leominster and Fitchburg were started during a presidential campaign that pitted Democrat Adlai Stevenson against the Republican nominee and war hero General Dwight David Eisenhower. Eisenhower's campaign slogan, which included his popular nickname, was "I like Ike."

Ike himself was an impassioned football player in his youth. Smallish and possessed of no great talent, the scrappy Eisenhower more than made up for his deficiencies with pure aggression that he brought to his playing days as a West Point Cadet. In 1912, the Carlisle Indian School and its legendary player Jim Thorpe came to face the Cadets at Callum Field. Carlisle Coach "Pop" Warner knew the importance of a game that showcased a competition between the powerful Cadets and Indians. Carlisle played for respect and dignity both on and, perhaps more importantly, off the gridiron. Warner understood his players, and before he sent them onto the field, he reminded them of some recent history. Could there be any greater motivation for a football contest than to remind the Indian players that their fathers and grandfathers were killed in the Indian wars by the fathers and grandfathers of the Cadets they would soon face? The Carlisle School beat the Cadets 27–6, and in the process, Ike hurt his knee badly attempting to sandwich the mighty Thorpe between himself and another army linebacker, Hobbs. Unfortunately for the army duo, Thorpe paused and watched the Cadets impact each other before gaining a few more yards. The injury, which was aggravated in future games, nearly ended Eisenhower's military career long before the fateful days of World War II.

Nevertheless, Ike maintained a deep interest in football throughout his life and was a good friend of Leominster's Lou Little. The two maintained a correspondence and as president, Ike is credited for convincing Coach Little to stay on at Columbia when other coaching opportunities arose. In the autumn of 1952, Eisenhower's focus was on winning the election and ending the war in Korea.

---

95   *Fitchburg Sentinel*, December 1, 1933.

The Leominster gridders of 1952 had an eye on the football field, but the war was an undeniable part of their lives. The enormity of it all was brought home by the loss of a native son in May. Sergeant William "Chalk" Antonucci, who quarterbacked the Blue and White just three seasons before, died in a plane crash while serving his country in Korea. He was nineteen years old. He left behind a family, a young brother who idolized him, a girl, and a community's memories. They remembered the young boy, not yet in high school, who tended the family's dog "Skippy," Leominster's unofficial mascot during football games. They remembered Number 17, who quarterbacked the Blue and White over Fitchburg 26–20 in 1949. But most of all, they lamented a life cut short, a future that would never be.

The 1952 season began and was played in a time of war and loss. The young men who graduated from high schools more than a decade before faced uncertainties that dwarfed the importance of sporting contests. But Americans carried on, as Americans always do, and the rivalry between Leominster and Fitchburg persevered.

The Blue and White fielded a talented team in 1952, and before Eisenhower was elected president on November 4, their record stood at 5–0–1, the only blemish being a 7–7 tie with Watertown in the season's second game. LHS played two more games before Thanksgiving, resulting in victories over Athol and Gardner. The Blue and White outscored their pre-Thanksgiving opponents 247–17. Fitchburg entered the traditional fray with a far less impressive 3–5 record.

Leominster's record would be preserved. LHS prevailed on Thanksgiving, beating Fitchburg 20–7. The 1952 gridders would have the distinction, which stands until today, of being the only LHS undefeated team whose record included a tie. The other four LHS undefeateds (1910, 1932, 1974, and 1978) all had perfect records.

Deadlocks aside, the Blue and White accomplished what they had to do on Thanksgiving Day. Quarterbacked by Angelo "Chubby" Celli, the Blue and White ground game rolled up 255 yards to their opponent's forty-seven and earned nineteen first downs while permitting Fitchburg two. Fullback Dick Surette scored two of Leominster's touchdowns and 140-pound right halfback Ronnie Saudelli scored the third.

Reporters besieged the winning coach, who was uncharacteristically calm as he picked up gear on the LHS sideline. Coach Broderick endorsed the idea of a post-season game for a team he deemed the most talented he ever coached at Leominster. Fitchburg's head coach, Marty McDonough, praised the winners and his own team for playing to the end. Fitchburg's linebacker, Bruce Smith, was awarded the Bernard W. St. Germaine trophy, as Fitchburg's outstanding Thanksgiving game player. Smith was the third recipient of the award created by the family of its namesake to honor their son, a former FHS lineman, who was killed in World War II.

A Coach Retires and a Team Battles To Stay Unbeaten, 1964

Thirty-four autumns have come and, but for a final Thanksgiving game, had gone. Coach Broderick was ready to hang up his cleats. A single game remained. Broderick took his team on a short bus ride to Crocker Field on a wet Thanksgiving morning to meet an unbeaten FHS team. Leominster's fortunes were not nearly as good. The "Comb-City" eleven posted but three wins against eight losses and were clear underdogs.

Crocker Field welcomed its traditional rivals. Veterans from Leominster teams of the early twenties, Henry Simard and John Kelley, arrived early and reminisced with other players of the era, Joe Toolin and Wayne Schell. The quartet was joined by attorney Isadore "Izzy" Solomon, who led cheers for LHS in 1925. On that day, Leominster cheerleaders carried a banner reading "All Leominster Says Thank You Charlie Broderick."

Fitchburg took to its home field, led by its star left halfback, tri-captain and triple threat Warren Muir, who scored all twenty points in a Fitchburg victory over Leominster the prior season. Characteristic of many Thanksgiving contests before and since, the unexpected thing happened. Fitchburg fell behind. Despite an impressive eleven-play drive resulting in six points, the Red and Gray ended the first half of play down 8–6 when Leominster quarterback Dave Horgan plunged into the Fitchburg end zone and the halfback, Roger Mercier, passed the ball to end Louis Giorgi for the successful conversion.

The teams retired from the soggy field for the shelter of the Crocker Field House and a halftime speech. The halftime break was a little longer than expected. Coach Broderick had a final maneuver in his coaching arsenal, and what he was precisely thinking is nothing more than speculation. Broderick had his team change out of soaked blue jerseys into dry white ones. The *Fitchburg Sentinel* theorized that the crafty coach simply intended a delay that dulled the impact of Fitchburg Coach Stan Goode's inspirational halftime words. (The Blue and White were forced to change back into their blue jerseys by rule that prohibited the visiting team's colors from conflicting with that of the home team—Fitchburg was already wearing white.) Perhaps, though, Broderick recalled a legendary tactic practiced by iconic Coach Clarence Amiott when he changed his Fitchburg squad into dry uniforms at halftime on the way to a 1936 FHS 7–6 victory on a Crocker Field quagmire.

Once questions over attire were settled, the teams finally got back to business. The third quarter featured a lack of offense by both teams with the home team managing but one of its total thirteen first downs and the visiting team netting just two of its total eight first downs. The Crocker Field faithful fretted anxiously and the Leominster fans, initially saddened by pregame predictions, had come to life. The fourth quarter settled things. On its first possession of the final stanza, the Red and Gray engineered a sixty-yard drive that featured runs of eleven, twenty, five, four, and two yards by Muir, punctuated by a final two-yard sweep to pay dirt. Muir celebrated by tossing the football into the covered grandstand at Crocker Field. Muir's rush for the conversion was repulsed, and the score stood FHS 12, LHS 8.

Leominster would have two more possessions, both ending in turnovers: first, a fumble recovered by the talented Muir, and the second, an interception by Fitchburg's Steve Bedard. Fitchburg survived the day and completed its season undefeated 7–0–2. The retiring coach tipped his hat to Muir and the Fitchburg squad and smiled broadly as he made an unannounced after-game visit to the FHS club. The Fitchburg team, who first knelt in silent prayer upon retiring to the lockers, put their coach and his assistants, Marco Landon and Jack Conway, through a ritual shower. The three men, soaked but elated, puffed on victory cigars. Coach Landon quipped, "I knew Leominster wouldn't quit—I knew they would stay right in there."[96] Landon spoke for his team—they would not have wanted it any other way.

A Classic Game and an Anniversary, 1969

Two men met at midfield on the Devil emblem, which was framed by a square of powder blue paint, and exchanged remarks. Twenty-two years earlier, they had stood together on Doyle Field as teammates. On a cold Thanksgiving Day in 1947, their Leominster team was defeated by Fitchburg, 13–0. But on Thursday, November 27, 1969, they met as opposing coaches in the annual Thanksgiving clash. Leon "Huck" Hannigan, referred to by his class yearbook as "diminutive but mighty ... a second (Doc) Blanchard," was Leominster's coach. His former classmate, Marco Landon, billed by the same yearbook as possessing "personality plus" and "leadership,"[97] was putting the latter characteristic to use as Fitchburg's head coach.

The contest was billed as a "David and Goliath" match, the vaunted Fitchburg eleven taking on the persona of the giant with their perfect 8–0 record. Leominster was a small but scrappy team that had clawed itself to a 6–2 mark, having lost to its two New Hampshire opponents, Nashua and Manchester. Not many local football pundits gave LHS a chance. Despite being tagged as a decided underdog, Coach Hannigan told his old friend Marco Landon that he was "sorry to have to ruin his undefeated season" as the two met just before the game got underway.[98]

The game was conceded to be the seventy-fifth anniversary of the rivalry. I suggest conceded, only because it was the first year the *Fitchburg Sentinel* recorded past game results, starting with the 1894 contest, as opposed to 1895. Why did that change in 1969? It could have been simply the recognition of the anniversary or the research and resulting piece written by Leominster Assistant Principal John Joyce that so eloquently chronicled that "first" 1894 contest in the game program prepared for the 1969 game. In any case, the stage was set

---

96   *Fitchburg Sentinel,* November 27, 1964.
97   Leominster High School Yearbook, 1948.
98   Celli and Piermarini, *The Rivalry.*

for a special game before a packed Doyle Field on a sunny but cold Thanksgiving Day.

The *Fitchburg Sentinel* featured an open letter by Robert Palmer, secretary of the Fitchburg High School All Sports Club, in its game coverage the evening before. Palmer noted, "We all know records don't count much tomorrow, when you meet those Blue Devils … you may be heroes … or absolutely nothing … too much depends on chance, luck, weather or how the ball bounces. What really counts is what you do."[99] If Palmer was prophetic, it seems the Leominster boys were listening more intently. The game was not decided by records but simply the play on the field.

The Blue and White played inspired football in a game that many consider to be one of the greatest upsets in the history of the series. Through the beneficence of a series of relatives and friends, my dad and I were treated to the press-box seats given annually to Ms. Louise Doyle, daughter of the donor of that field. From the perch of the gray-clad press box, the panorama of the game unfolded. Leominster took charge from the opening kickoff, marching the ball sixty-two yards to the first score of the game. Fitchburg's first possession and drive was halted when sophomore Eric Legere intercepted an Allen Glenny pass that Leominster capitalized on, with a drive which ended with a Jim DePasquale's thirty-two-yard run for the Leominster second touchdown and a 13–0 lead. After Fitchburg was forced to punt, Leominster's third possession also resulted in points when right halfback Robert Metivier hauled in a Michael Caisse pass for a forty-five-yard scoring play. Leominster led at the half, 19–0.

The second half featured offense from both squads; however, again, led by the stellar play of its backfield, which included Metivier, DePasquale, Jim Giadone, quarterback Michael Caisse, and fullback Tom Caisse. LHS outscored the Red and Gray 21–18. When the final whistle sounded, Leominster fans celebrated wildly, taking with them a convincing 40–18 upset and any hopes for Fitchburg's third undefeated season.[100]

---

99 *Fitchburg Sentinel*, November 26, 1969.

100 Fitchburg's third undefeated season finally came in 2000 when that squad posted a perfect record twelve victories.

Dramatic Contests of Remarkable Contrast, 1978 and 1993

In the wake of each match, fans of both Leominster and Fitchburg left the field confident they had witnessed a game for the ages. The Thanksgiving game played on Crocker Field in 1978 was a defensive contest played on a frigid day. In 1993, the holiday classic visited Doyle Field and featured an epic display of offense. Both games were filled with drama. In each case, the outcome was in doubt until the final play. In 1978 and 1993, the fans of both high schools held their breath in nervous anticipation while witnessing all the theatrics that the game of football can provide. If you sift through the 126 Leominster-Fitchburg games played since 1894, these two games, while polar opposites, would exemplify the richness of a rivalry steeped in the unexpected and the spectacular.

Thursday, November 23, 1978

Thanksgiving Day 1978 dawned cold and gray. Frozen Crocker Field was dusted with snow, and welcomed fans bundled against the cold. Each city's faithful had high expectations for their team, and each squad had enjoyed considerable success that year. Leominster's mission was simple: win and complete an undefeated season. Fitchburg suffered but one defeat in 1978, losing to Nashua High School by a score of 30–27. Each squad displayed a potent offense that year, and the expectation was for a high-scoring game.

Things could not have worked out more differently. Frank Novak, wearing Number 15, lined up a kick. The senior heard admonitions from the sideline, "Keep your head down; keep your head down." Earlier in the contest, Novak had attempted a field goal that failed, and somehow he had to maintain his focus on a second attempt. The game was in overtime. Four quarters of regulation football had not produced a single point. Leominster made six deep incursions into Fitchburg territory, and each time, the Red and Gray defense rose up and repelled the Blue and White invaders. Fitchburg never stepped foot into Leominster territory, managing but 136 yards of total offense. The game would be decided by the interscholastic tie-breaker system.

Under this system, still in effect today, each team is afforded four downs from their opponent's ten-yard line to score. The score after each team has its opportunity is the final score. Most coaches winning the overtime coin toss would prefer to take the ball last, sending their defense onto the field first to seal at least a tie, or more optimistically, hand their offense the ball with an opportunity for victory by scoring either a touchdown or a field goal.

Fitchburg won the coin toss and opted to defend first. Leominster's first three attempts netted six yards, and the Blue and White had one final attempt to score with the ball at the Fitchburg four-yard line. Leominster Coach Peter Beaulieu sent in his kicker, confident in his decision despite Novak's earlier miss. The game, Leominster's undefeated season, and the hopes of fans all hung in the balance. Senior Chris Daigneault received the snap and with one fluid motion got the ball in position for his kicker. Novak had time. He remembered "keep your head down" as he kicked through the ball. The twenty-one-yard field goal attempt was good. Leominster had finally put points on the scoreboard. The task now fell to the Blue and White defense.

The contest was decided on Fitchburg's fourth and final down. On the preceding attempt, Fitchburg's quarterback, Kevin Conway, ran an option to the left side instead of the expected dive by the big, bruising fullback, Todd Becker. Conway nearly scored, missing the opportunity by inches. The ball was spotted one foot from Leominster's end zone. The final snap brought the expected. Becker took the hand off, slashing at the Leominster front. The Blue and White line of Joe Veneziano, Lewis Austin, Jay Arsenault, and David Brow didn't budge, stopping Becker short of the goal.

Leominster fans experienced pure jubilation, made all the more dramatic by the long struggle and climactic ending. It would be difficult to write a more fitting end to an undefeated season, the exclamation point of which was victory in one of the sport's most ancient of rivalries. It was the last of five undefeated seasons achieved by the Blue and White to date, all of those seasons—1910, 1932, 1952, 1974, and 1978—being perfect, unbeaten, untied campaigns, except 1952. In stark contrast, the mood was sullen and somber in the Fitchburg locker room. Coach David Horgan absorbed the loss, calling it the "biggest ... of (his) entire life."[101]

It wasn't just a close game but a shared tragedy among a group of players who found a deep emotional bond. Tri-captain James Pappas, who suffered a season-ending injury before he could play a down of his senior season, was the team's emotional leader. What he couldn't do on the field was more than made up for in the post-game locker room that day. Pappas's words of devotion preserved his team's pride and the strength of its common purpose when his teammates needed it most.

Thursday, November 25, 1993

The sunshine of Thanksgiving 1993 brought an offensive display to Doyle Field unequalled in the long history of the rivalry. Before it was over, the game yielded 872 yards of total offense, twelve touchdowns, and eighty-four total points. Fitchburg Coach Ray Cosenza, who "had to look at the scoreboard again," still views the contest as the greatest he has ever witnessed.[102] As much as 1978 was a defensive struggle, 1993 was a battle waged by two heavyweights trading unrelenting blow for blow with no clear hint at who would remain standing.

In what will forever be one of the series' most outstanding efforts, Leominster's quarterback Bob Raxasack accounted for 347 total yards and had a hand in all of Leominster's forty points. Raxasack threw for 223 yards, going eight of seventeen passing, and ran nine times for seventy-nine yards and two touchdowns. The talented quarterback also contributed on special teams, scoring on a forty-five-yard punt return and kicking four extra points. Never will a Leominster football player compile those kind of statistics in a losing effort.

The fourth quarter of the 1993 chapter of the rivalry featured five lead changes. With less than a minute remaining, Fitchburg trailed 40–36. The Red and Gray quarterback, Todd Steffanides, rolled left first, reading Leominster's short coverage, which was closing. Steffanides quickly picked up wide receiver James McCall, who was separating from the Leominster deep coverage. The quarterback connected with McCall on a thirty-four-yard scoring play. Tailback Ryan Keenan

---

101 *Fitchburg Sentinel*, November 24, 1978.
102 *Fitchburg Sentinel*, November 26, 1993.

added a two-point conversion, and Fitchburg regained the lead 44–40 with but thirty seconds left. None of the seven thousand fans in attendance thought the game was over. One side of Doyle Field was about to experience the longest thirty seconds of their lives and the other a "New York" half minute.

Without any timeouts left, Leominster took possession of the ball. On the first snap, Raxasack took his drop and threw a bullet to split end Bryan Mazzaferro, breaking over the middle near midfield. Mazzaferro headed for the left sideline with the Leominster throng urging him on. Mazzaferro outran strong safety Ryan Keenan as the Blue and White fans prayed for fleetness of foot. From across the field sped Zack McCall. The Fitchburg safety made one of the greatest tackles in the history of the rivalry, downing Mazzaferro on the Fitchburg three-yard line with seventeen seconds left. The Leominster offense hurried to the line and Raxasack spiked the ball, preserving one last chance for the Blue and White. It was the opportunity the fans had hoped for less than a minute earlier. One more play for victory. The play was called, one that had succeeded throughout the day. Raxasack handed off to halfback John Miller on a dive over left tackle. Miller fought his way to the one-yard line, where he was stalled. In that last instant, in the peal of the final whistle, a titanic clash ended. The Fitchburg fans celebrated, and their coach looked up at the scoreboard in disbelief for confirmation. Coach Cosenza had just led the Red and Gray to a victory that will always be an important part of the texture of the rivalry. Today, the 1993 installment still reigns supreme as the one game—of 125 played thus far—with the most total points scored. Fittingly, it was a game that took every play to decide the outcome.

Afterword

On Saturday, November 22, 1906, George Wise, Fitchburg's football team captain, started on a twenty-yard run with the ball tucked tightly under his arm. The opposing quarterback lay in wait and timed his hard tackle. Wise hit the ground with force, and the violent downing resulted in a broken collarbone. The *Fitchburg Sentinel* announced on Wednesday, November 26 that Captain Wise would not be available for the Thanksgiving game with Leominster the following day. Wise would have to wait an entire year for his chance at Leominster. When that opportunity came in 1907, Wise made the best of it. His dramatic last-minute field goal tied the game before a record crowd at Leominster's old athletic grounds. That Thanksgiving contest in particular captured the attention of both communities. Excitement for the rivalry was at an all-time high.

In the 114 years that have passed since the high schools of Leominster and Fitchburg embarked on their compilation of football history, the years and decades have captured drama both on and off the football field. From the earliest years, each decade, each year produced players and participants who nobly faced challenges posed by both football and life. Early on, the Leominster-Fitchburg rivalry became a stage on which to demonstrate courage and sacrifice for team and community. Each squad welcomed the competition, but not because they were counterparts or foes. No, each community sent its high school football team to the gridiron hoping for superlative competition; without the best of opposition, nothing could be proved. As the years passed, each school could rely on one thing from the other—the very best effort regardless of the odds, prior record, size, experience, or talent. Each would come to play, and seasons would be measured on the result regardless of relative successes or failures that came in earlier games that autumn.

With the passing decades, tradition became a shorthand for these notions that early players had an intuition for. When Mark O'Toole stepped onto the gridiron at Leominster driving park in October 1894, he could not have predicted that four generations of his family would play football in a rivalry he was helping to start that very day. He could not have predicted the scores of players who would become local football legends any more than he could predict which among these young men would make courageous contributions off the football field, including his son and namesake Mark K. O'Toole, an army pilot who died when his plane crashed during World War II.

The rivalry has produced an unending chain of successes and failures, years of triumph and painful losses. What the rivalry has never produced is a sense of quit in either team. Both high schools make their annual appearance on the gridiron with all the enthusiasm and all the fire that their opponent has grown to expect and welcome. The tradition of Leominster and Fitchburg was born and continues simply because each team can rely on the other to provide the perfect stage, the perfect opponent for a battle of gallantry and glory.

Into this annual quest to take honor from the field is woven a texture of human experience that layers the history of the rivalry. The lives of the participants are sometimes inseparable from exploits on the football field. In some cases, the rivalry was a launching point, an opportunity to demonstrate an ability to act under pressure and gain the notoriety that only the big game can bring.

On Thanksgiving morning 1968, Fitchburg High School faced the prospect of playing the annual contest with Leominster without the services of their starting quarterback, Chris Petrides, who was injured just days before. Fitchburg's Coach Marco Landon would look to his junior backup quarterback to lead the Red and Gray in the most important game of the year. Coach Landon's confidence was well placed. Allen Glenny led Fitchburg High School to a 16–14 victory over Leominster and won the St. Germaine Trophy as Fitchburg's most valuable player. In 1969, Glenny led a powerful Red and Gray squad to an 8–0 record before being upset by Leominster on Thanksgiving Day.

Following graduation from FHS, Glenny earned an appointment to the U.S. Naval Academy at Annapolis, Maryland. He played four years of football for Navy, starting at quarterback in both his junior and senior years. As Navy's starting quarterback, Glenny broke a number of school records, some of which belonged to Heisman Trophy winner Roger Staubach. In 1973, Glenny was awarded the outstanding player trophy in the Army-Navy game, which the midshipmen won by a score of 51–0.

Glenny entered Naval Flight School after completing his years at Annapolis, following his dream to become a navy flyer. Lieutenant Allen Glenny had long been following his dreams since his youthful days on Crocker Field. By any measure, he has achieved much. On April 18, 1980, Lieutenant Glenny piloted a P-3 Orion Antisubmarine Aircraft in connection with American Samoa's Eightieth Flag Day celebration. Just before 10:00 AM, the plane made two passes over Page Harbor, dropping six skydivers from the Army's Tropical Lightning Parachute Club of Hawaii for the entertainment of the holiday crowd. On the third pass, the plane struck a cable suspending an aerial tramway and crashed, killing the pilot, Lieutenant Glenny, and the other five crewmen.

Lieutenant Glenny's example captures all of the elements of the rivalry. He answered the call when his team needed him and performed with courage and grace. The lessons learned on the high school gridiron were magnified when Lieutenant Glenny's contribution was for his country. Like so many others who have participated in the rivalry, he understood what it meant to be involved in something bigger than any individual who ever took part in the game. The game is and always will be bigger than any player, regardless of the size or quality of the contribution. In the end, it is for this reason that the rivalry will continue and persevere as it has for more than eleven decades.

In a century from now, the inhabitants of Fitchburg and Leominster will look back to an even more faded origin of their rivalry. In that distant time, it will become even more difficult to appreciate that the annual rite was neither inevitable nor always firmly rooted. Future witnesses will, however, continue to understand that the tradition of Leominster and Fitchburg is something special, not easily duplicated. It will always transcend a player, a team, or one game. In this notion, we can all find one constant in a world of turbulence and change.

Table of Games

(1893–2008)

Year	Team	Score		Year	Team	Score
1893	Leominster	8–6 *		1918	Fitchburg	20–0
1894	Leominster	40–0		1919	Fitchburg	12–0
1895	Fitchburg	14–6		1920	Fitchburg	35–7
1896	Fitchburg	18–0		1921	Tie	7–7
1897	Fitchburg	4–0		1922	Fitchburg	12–6
1897	Fitchburg	8–0		1924	Fitchburg	48–0
1898	Leominster	5–0		1925	Leominster	9–0
1898	Tie	0–0 **		1926	Fitchburg	20–0
1899	Fitchburg	10–0		1927	Fitchburg	64–0
1899	Tie	0–0		1928	Leominster	6–3
1901	Fitchburg	7–0		1929	Leominster	6–0
1901	Leominster	5–0		1930	Fitchburg	6–0
1903	Leominster	6–0		1931	Fitchburg	24–7
1903	Tie	0–0		1932	Leominster	25–0
1904	Fitchburg	46–0		1933	Fitchburg	20–12
1904	Fitchburg	48–0		1934	Leominster	14–0
1905	Fitchburg	10–0		1935	Fitchburg	33–14
1906	Fitchburg	17–0		1936	Fitchburg	7–6
1907	Tie	4–4		1937	Leominster	26–6
1908	Fitchburg	2–0		1938	Leominster	14–0
1909	Fitchburg	5–0		1939	Leominster	18–0
1910	Leominster	6–0		1940	Leominster	6–0
1910	Leominster	23–0		1941	Fitchburg	14–6
1911	Leominster	9–0		1942	Leominster	25–7
1911	Leominster	17–0		1943	Leominster	13–6
1912	Tie	0–0		1944	Leominster	26–0
1912	Leominster	19–0		1945	Tie	6–6
1913	Tie	0–0		1946	Fitchburg	7–6
1913	Fitchburg	13–0		1947	Fitchburg	13–0
1914	Fitchburg	27–0		1948	Fitchburg	13–7
1914	Fitchburg	33–0		1949	Leominster	26–20
1915	Fitchburg	62–0		1950	Leominster	19–13
1915	Fitchburg	13–0		1951	Fitchburg	12–0
1916	Fitchburg	49–0		1952	Leominster	20–7
1916	Fitchburg	27–0		1953	Leominster	7–0
1917	Fitchburg	42–0		1954	Leominster	27–7

1955	Leominster	39–7	1982	Leominster	41–6
1956	Leominster	44–13	1983	Leominster	28–12
1957	Fitchburg	20–14	1984	Fitchburg	29–2
1958	Fitchburg	24–10	1985	Leominster	13–6
1959	Tie	0–0	1986	Leominster	23–15
1960	Tie	14–14	1987	Leominster	20–6
1961	Leominster	26–12	1988	Leominster	25–8
1962	Leominster	14–0	1989	Leominster	29–6
1963	Fitchburg	20–0	1990	Leominster	27–0
1964	Fitchburg	12–8	1991	Fitchburg	14–0
1965	Leominster	27–0	1992	Fitchburg	14–13
1966	Leominster	14–12	1993	Fitchburg	44–40
1967	Leominster	16–0	1994	Fitchburg	38–14
1968	Fitchburg	16–14	1995	Fitchburg	38–6
1969	Leominster	40–18	1996	Fitchburg	28–19
1970	Leominster	14–12	1997	Leominster	26–8
1971	Fitchburg	12–7	1998	Fitchburg	21–7
1972	Fitchburg	27–19	1999	Fitchburg	38–21
1973	Leominster	15–0	2000	Fitchburg	28–6
1974	Leominster	36–13	2001	Fitchburg	26–14
1975	Leominster	19–0	2002	Fitchburg	28–20
1976	Leominster	38–22	2003	Fitchburg	24–14
1977	Leominster	7–0	2004	Leominster	19–14
1978	Leominster	3–0	2005	Leominster	20–6
1979	Leominster	34–6	2006	Leominster	34–6
1980	Leominster	43–8	2007	Leominster	14–13
1981	Leominster	27–12	2008	Fitchburg	20–17

* Not included in series standing or point totals since the game is loosely categorized as a high school match. This game occurred in conjunction with the Leominster Cattle Show on Wednesday, September 13, 1893. Another game between the Fitchburgs and the Leominsters later in November of that year ended with Fitchburg dominating. Neither the score of that game nor the composition of the team is known.

** The *Fitchburg Sentinel* account claims this game as a 5–0 Fitchburg victory; however, the game official ruled the game a scoreless tie. That result is included in the series standings and point totals.

Series Standings

Fitchburg - 58 wins
Leominster - 57 wins
Ties - 10
Points:
Fitchburg - 1,677
Leominster - 1,565

On Thanksgiving morning 2008, Fitchburg and Leominster High Schools met for the 125th time. At the conclusion of regulation time, the score was 17–17. More astounding was the tie the teams had achieved, neatly reflecting the series standings, each team having won fifty-seven of the prior contests with ten ending in a tie. Modern tie-breaking rules, non-existent in prior decades, resulted in an overtime session. Fitchburg was triumphant, having scored the lone points in overtime, a field goal.

The rivalry between Leominster and Fitchburg is remarkable not only for its age or number of games, but also for the resiliency of the communities and the teams they send to the gridiron each autumn. It is only fitting that this long football relationship could be absolutely deadlocked after 124 games and forty-eight minutes of regulation play. Could the young men who lined up for the first match in October of 1894 have predicted that?

The Author

Bibliography

I.   Archives

Crocker Field House, Fitchburg, Massachusetts

Fitchburg Historical Society, Fitchburg, Massachusetts

Leominster Historical Society, Leominster, Massachusetts

Leominster Public Library, Valuable Collection, Leominster,
    Massachusetts

II.   Primary Sources

Boston Journal (newspaper)

Fitchburg Sentinel (newspaper)

Leominster Enterprise (newspaper)

Fitchburg vs. Leominster, Thanksgiving Day Program, 1931

Leominster vs. Fitchburg, Thanksgiving Day Program, November 24,
    1949

Leominster vs. Fitchburg, Thanksgiving Day Program, November 27,
    1969

Program Dedication of Doyle Field, Saturday, October 10, 1931

Fitchburg High School Yearbook 1894

Fitchburg High School Yearbook 1896

Fitchburg High School Yearbook 1897

Fitchburg High School Yearbook 1898

Fitchburg High School Yearbook 1899

Fitchburg High School Yearbook 1900

Fitchburg High School Yearbook 1901

Fitchburg High School Yearbook 1902

Fitchburg High School Yearbook 1903

Fitchburg High School Yearbook 1904

Fitchburg High School Yearbook 1905

Fitchburg High School Yearbook 1906

Fitchburg High School Yearbook 1907

Fitchburg High School Yearbook 1908

Fitchburg High School Yearbook 1909

Fitchburg High School Yearbook 1910

Fitchburg High School Yearbook 1911

Fitchburg High School Yearbook 1912

Fitchburg High School Yearbook 1913

Fitchburg High School Yearbook 1914

Fitchburg High School Yearbook 1915

Fitchburg High School Yearbook 1916

Fitchburg High School Yearbook 1917

Fitchburg High School Yearbook 1918

Fitchburg High School Yearbook 1919

Football Notes of Michael Curley, circa 2007

The Boulder (Fitchburg High School Yearbook) 1932

The Boulder (Fitchburg High School Yearbook) 1933

The Boulder (Fitchburg High School Yearbook) 1934

The Leonine (Leominster High School Yearbook) 1926

The Leonine (Leominster High School Yearbook) 1927

The Magnet (Leominster High School Yearbook) 1930

The Magnet (Leominster High School Yearbook) 1931

The Magnet (Leominster High School Yearbook) 1948

The Owlet (Leominster High School Yearbook) 1904

Leominster Directory 1890–91, New Haven, Conn., The Price & Lee Co., 1890

Leominster Directory 1892–93, New Haven, Conn., The Price & Lee Co., 1892

Leominster Directory 1893–94, New Haven, Conn., The Price & Lee Co., 1893

Leominster Directory 1899–00, New Haven, Conn., The Price & Lee Co., 1899

Leominster Directory 1900–01, New Haven, Conn., The Price & Lee Co., 1900

Leominster Directory 1901–02, New Haven, Conn., The Price & Lee Co., 1901

Leominster Directory 1902–03, New Haven, Conn., The Price & Lee Co., 1902

Leominster Directory 1903–04, New Haven, Conn., The Price & Lee Co., 1903

Valuation of Estates and Taxes Assessed in the Town of Leominster for the Year 1890, Leominster, Massachusetts, C.H. Hyatt, Enterprise Office, 1890.

Valuation of Estates and Taxes Assessed in the Town of Leominster for the Year 1891, Leominster, Massachusetts, C.H. Hyatt, Enterprise Office, 1891.

Valuation of Estates and Taxes Assessed in the Town of Leominster for the Year 1892, Leominster, Massachusetts, C.H. Hyatt, Enterprise Office, 1892.

Valuation of Estates and Taxes Assessed in the Town of Leominster for the Year 1893, Leominster, Massachusetts, C.H. Hyatt, Enterprise Office, 1893.

Valuation of Estates and Taxes Assessed in the Town of Leominster for the Year 1894, Leominster, Massachusetts, C.H. Hyatt, Enterprise Office, 1894.

III.   Books

Anderson, Lars. 2007 *Carlisle vs. Army*. New York: Random House

Brinkley, Douglas. 1998. *History of the United States*. New York: Viking Penguin

Brooks, Philip L. 2007. *Forward Pass.* Yardley, Pennsylvania: Westholme Publishing

Camp, Walter. 1891. *American Football.* New York: Harper & Brothers

Camp, Walter and Deland, Lorin F. 1896. *Football.* Cambridge, Massachusetts: Houghton, Mifflin and Company

Doyle, Bernard W. 1925. *Comb Making in America.* Leominster, Massachusetts: privately published

Edwards, Lieut. Frank E. 1899. *The '98 Campaign of the 6th Massachusetts U.S.V.* Boston: Little Brown and Company

Emerson, William A. 1888. *Leominster Historical and Picturesque.* Gardner, Massachusetts: Lithotype Publishing Co.

Kirkpatrick, Doris. 1971. *The City and the River.* Fitchburg, Massachusetts: Fitchburg Historical Society

Kirkpatrick, Doris. 1975. *Around the World in Fitchburg.* Fitchburg, Fitchburg Historical Society

Little, Lou, and Arthur Sampson. 1934. *Lou Little's Football.* Leominster, Massachusetts: Leominster Printing Co.

Maggio, Frank P. 2007. *Notre Dame and the Game That Changed Football.* New York: Carroll & Graff Publishers

Nelson, David M. 1994. *The Anatomy of a Game.* Wilmington, Delaware: University of Delaware Press

Oates Jr., Bob, Editor, 1969. *The First Fifty Years: The Story of the National Football League,* New York: Simon & Schuster

Reid, Bill, and Ronald A. Smith 1994. *Big Time Football at Harvard 1905: The Diary of Coach Bill Reid.* Champaign, Illinois: Illinois Press

Time-Life Books. 1970. *This Fabulous Century,* vol. 1870-1900. New York: Time, Inc.

Watterson, John Sayle. 2002. *College Football.* Baltimore: JHU Press

Weyand, A.M. 1926. *American Football. Its History And Development.* New York and London: D. Appleton & Company

Whittingham, Richard. 2001. *Rites of Autumn*. New York: The Free Press

Wilder, David. 1853. *The History of Leominster*. Fitchburg, Massachusetts: Fitchburg Reveille

IV.   Additional Sources

Needham, Henry Beach. "Unnecessary Roughness." *McClure's Magazine 25* (July 1905).

Watkins, John Elfreth, Jr. "What May Happen in the Next Hundred Years." *Ladies Home Journal* 18 (December 1900).

Bill Reid '01 Harvard's First Pioneer for Athletics, http:www.varsityclub. harvard.edu/newsviews/volume46/issuetwo/46reidtwo.htm.

Chronology of Football Rule Changes, http://www.huskies.se/index.php.

Football as we know it c. 1906, http://divisionoflabour.com/ archives/002129.php.

On American Football, c. 1906, http://divisionoflabour.com/ archives/002931.php.

Rule Changes Throughout the History of College Football, http:// homepages.cae.wisc.edu/~dwilson/rstc/RuleChanges.txt.

The Rivalry, DVD. Directed and produced by Jack Celli and Carl Piermarini, Leominster, MA, originally released in 1983 and updated 2005. Piermacelli Films, Inc.

Watterson, John S., "Out of Baseball's Shadow: The Paradox of College Football Scholarship," *Journal of Sports History* 29, no. 2, (Summer 2002).

Index

Page numbers in **bold** indicate photos.

Breinigsville, PA USA
18 September 2009
224332BV00001B/9/P